WAY OF THE RAVEN

WARRIOR SCOUT

VOLUME THREE
SPECIAL EDITION

A collaborative series between

Benjamin Raven Pressley & Fernan Vargas

OFFERED BY

AND

WAY OF THE RAVEN

WARRIOR SCOUT

VOLUME THREE

By Benjamin Raven Pressley & Fernan Vargas

Cover Model: Steven M. Watts
Photo Models:
Benjamin Raven Presley, German Dominguez, Fernan Vargas,
Adam Nunez, David Woulard & Manley Blackman

Copyright©2017
by
Fernan Vargas and Benjamin Raven Pressley
All rights reserved.

The authors and publishers of this manual accept no liability whatsoever for any injuries to persons or property resulting from applications or adoption of any of these procedures, considerations or tactics presented or implied in this text. This training manual is not designed or intended to function as a self-teaching manual of techniques. This course is to be taught by a certified instructor and the manual is only a training aid used for reference. No part of this book may be reproduced in any form or by any means without permission, in writing from the Authors.

ISBN-13:978-1983778971
ISBN-10:1983778974

DEDICATION

This book is dedicated to
Steven M. Watts
July 25, 1947-March 21, 2016

This volume is dedicated to Steven M. Watts. One of my greatest mentors. He was a teacher, philosopher, craftsman, lifelong boy scout, artist, interpreter, author, poet, philanthropist, musician, advocate, historian, movie and television consultant, pirate, cowboy, clown, loving husband, father and grandfather, and everyone's favorite teacher. He affected many lives literally worldwide. His love and passion for the preservation and teaching of primitive skills was unmatched. I caught fire with primitive skills when I met him. He is mostly responsible for putting me on the path I am now practicing and teaching primitive and survival skills. Steve had a way of placing skills he taught into an anthropological matrix that emphasized not just teaching skills for skills sake but how they fit into all our biological and anthropological DNA so to speak. He inspired me early on as to how the past unites all human beings for there was a time in all our histories that we used stone age skills. He is an amazing communicator, teacher, author and continues to have a profound effect on who I am and how I teach. I can't thank Steve enough for being part of my life.---***Benjamin Raven Pressley***

FOREWORD

Congratulations! You have made it to volume three of the Warrior Scout series! I hope you are enjoying it and benefitting from it as much as we are and as much as we hope you do. This series is unique in its presentation and combination of self-defense, survival skills and warrior philosophy. It is timely and much needed information for the times we live in and the times to come. Warriors of old knew how to be prepared. They practiced their skills during times of war or peace. It should be the same today for the modern day warrior. You may be blessed enough to live in a country where you enjoy relative safety and peace like we experience in the United States of America. However, the true warrior will not become drunk on the peace and safety he enjoys. The true warrior knows there is still turmoil going on underneath the surface and behind the scenes. The ocean is a view of serenity and peace looking at it from the shore but beneath the surface are riptides that can carry away a swimmer and drown or dash him against the rocks, predators such as sharks that would gladly make a meal out of a wayward unaware swimmer or surfer and currents that travel across the surface of the entire globe. A true warrior knows how to draw peace and serenity in spite of his circumstances and point of vantage and knows to always be aware. Warrior Scout was written for the survivor and warrior in us all. In some cases to awaken the survivor and warrior, in some cases to keep the survivor and warrior sharp and at their best. Warrior Scout was written for you! The Scout of old was the point man. They led the way. They watched the trail for dangers. They defended those in their care. They had knowledge and skills that made them stand out and some appeared to be almost supernatural in their ways. They seemed to see better, be smarter and stronger than the average person. Stories and legends came to be of such people. But the truth was they were just like anyone else with one important difference they applied themselves to learning, they practiced their skills, they were students and teachers. They learned to draw from something deeper than the knowledge and training they received. They found that in the midst of the countless hours of training and learning that there was a wellspring of strength and courage deep within that could only have been known because they had prepared themselves. From this wellspring they had found deep within they could walk in the valley of the shadow of death unafraid and confident. This is our desire for you with the Warrior Scout series. Welcome to the tribe!

---*Benjamin 'Raven' Pressley*

WAY OF THE RAVEN

WARRIOR SCOUT

VOLUME THREE

TABLE OF CONTENTS

THE WARRIOR SCOUT DIPLOMA PROGRAM

The Warrior Scout series is more than a set of books. We believe it can change your life for the better. These volumes are the perfect combination of self-defense techniques, survival skills and warrior philosophy. Within these pages are inspiration and how to be the warrior in life we all need to be. Being a warrior is an honorable thing. It is a way of life that fits into and is so vital for everyday life. The Seven Virtues of Bushido sum up these principles well. The warrior is not just someone that fights on the battlefield it is someone who defends a way of life that is honorable and sustainable for all people, weak and strong.

THE SEVEN VIRTUES OF BUSHIDO

The scout historically was the point man. They blazed the trail. They walked into the jaws of the unknown and came back to report on what was ahead. They made sure the world ahead was a safe one as much as was possible for those in their charge.

There have always been warrior scouts among us. In darker times they were still there but often had to train underground, strike secretly, assess the situation, then lead the remnant that still believed in the seven virtues out of the darkness and into the light.

There still are warrior scouts among us who assess the weakness and danger in modern day society and choose to not walk in the ways of darkness or on a path that is not sustainable. They may not always stand out but that is not their intention to stand out. They wait and bide their time and step up when it is time to defend the innocent. They are fathers, mothers, sisters and brothers. They are elders, law enforcement and fire fighters. They are soldiers and they are everyday people who care about the world that is being left to their children. *They are you and me.*

We desire that you read these volumes with purpose. Practice the skills taught, ponder the truths brought forth. Then we wish to recognize your accomplishments. How? We have a workbook that will test your knowledge and help you apply what you have learned. Then we wish to recognize you with a diploma and welcome you to an elite group that we will offer many special offers, discounts and further training to in the future. To enroll and receive the workbook just contact us by e-mail at raven@wayoftheraven.net. Subject Line: Warrior Scout

SURVIVAL SKILLS

FOOD

Acquiring meat in the wild is so important to survival. Here is an easy way to catch crayfish that works very well: Take a bandanna and fill it with chicken livers or fish entrails and gather the corners and tie it shut. Tie a string to it and throw it in a stream where you know crayfish are. Come back later and you will have several crayfish clinging to the bandanna trying to get to the bait. Just gather them up and boil them alive. They are like little lobsters. The meatiest part is the tail. If they are large enough you can get meat from the claws. And before you discard the rest of the body break off the head and suck the flavor from it like the Cajuns do! This technique also works for crabs. Beware though shellfish and mollusks should not be eaten if the water they are in is polluted.

Traps and Snares

Acquiring meat may be done by trapping, snaring, fishing or hunting. Learn a few deadfall triggers and snares. It usually takes 25-50 traps and snares set out in an area to keep one person in meat. You don't just set one trap and get a rabbit in it everyday like portrayed in the movies, unless you're very lucky! Knowing what the animals in your area are eating and being able to detect game trails and properly placing your trap or snare and concealing the trap and your scent are very important. Sharp pointed sticks can be placed in an area where there are game trails with various baits on them. Leave them overnight and then check them the next morning and you will be able to tell what the animals are eating in your area and then you can bait your trap accordingly. Fencing a trap is also important in the case of deadfall traps. This is using natural materials surrounding all sides of your trap to direct an animal in the way you wish him to go. It also camouflages your trap well.

Other considerations to think about are that it is sometimes necessary to put a stone in the ground under the deadfall trap. Some animals are so soft boned that they may survive a trap falling on them in soft ground. Sometimes you even need to put a stone under the trigger to keep it from sinking into the ground. And beware of human scent on your trap. This can sometimes be avoided as easily as rubbing the string you use and other parts of the trap in the dirt.

Springpole Deadfall Trap. It combines a springpole with a deadfall trap that snatches the trigger when tripped.

Setting a Springpole Snare.

Running Snare

Figure 4 Deadfall Trap

Figure Four deadfall trap. Note rock laid into ground also. Some animals are soft boned and can survive a trap dropped on soft ground. Sometimes it is necessary to put a rock under the trigger also to keep it from sinking into ground.

The deadfall trap may also be used with birds but they will not crawl into a closed area. Rather than use a solid rock or log make an open cage-like box and bait the trap with something that will attract them.

Following are drawings to help you better understand these traps and snares and how they work.

FIGURE FOUR DEADFALL TRAP

By Benjamin Pressley

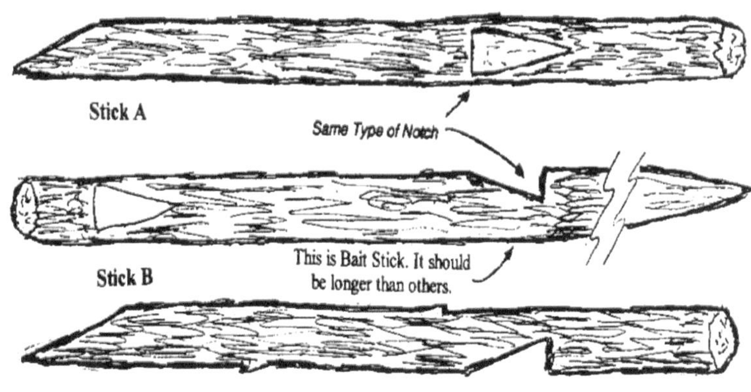

When carving notches periodically fit together to make sure all notches are lining up properly and a nice straight figure four is formed. Notches may be cut shallow to make trap more sensitive. As animal nibbles bait trigger gives way and animal is crushed by weight.

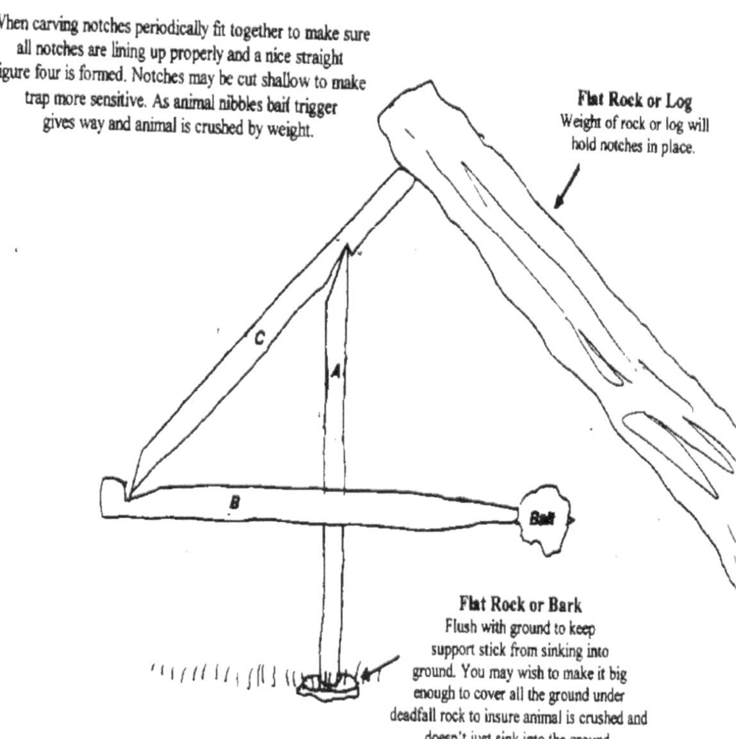

LIFT POLE SNARE

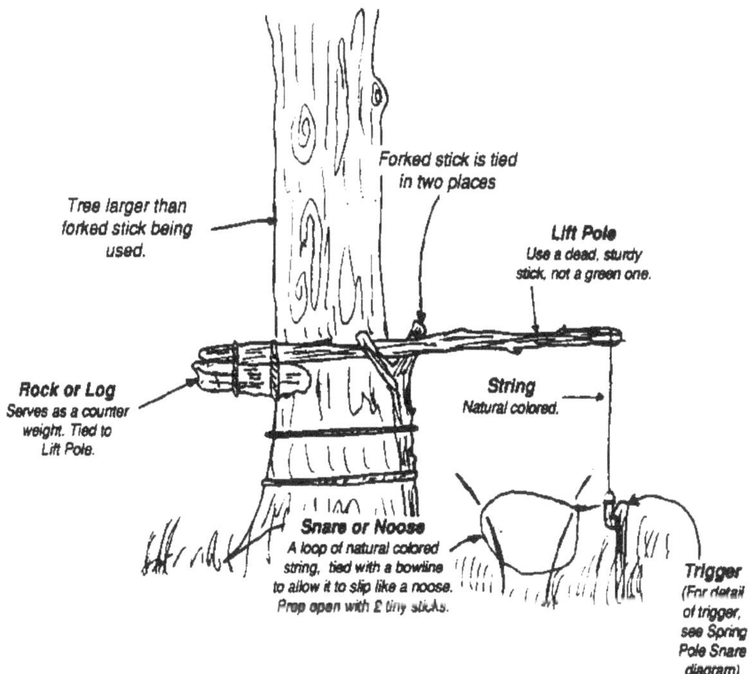

How It Works: *The Lift Pole Snare works, in principle, the same as the Spring Pole Snare, except when the trigger is sprung, the counter weight lifts the animal causing it to choke, due to the tightening of the noose around its neck. The Lift Pole may be used when a dead, springy stick is hard to find for a Spring Pole Snare and works just as well.*

SPRING POLE SNARE

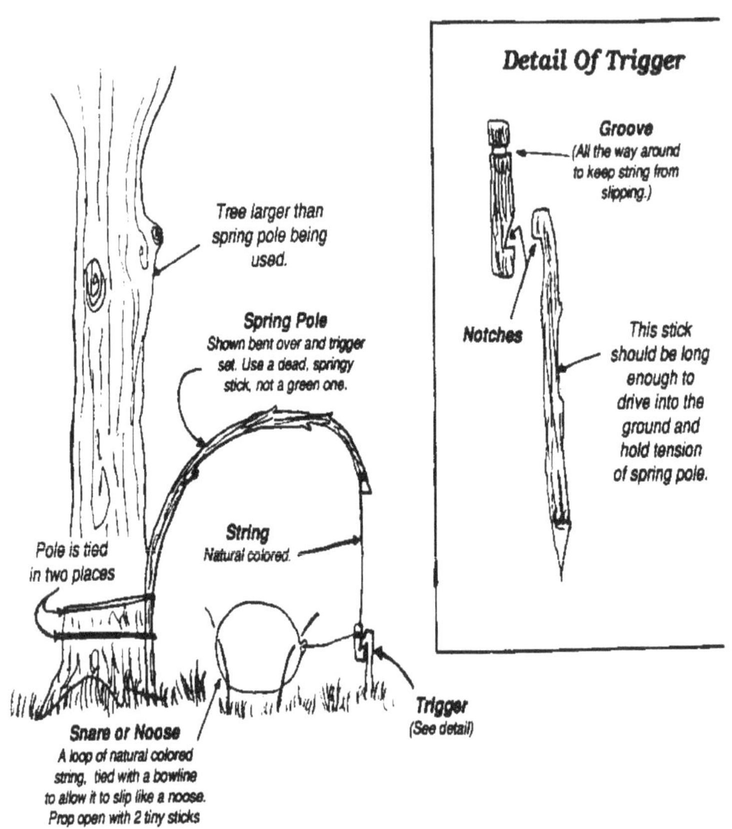

How It Works: *This snare is placed in a well worn animal trail. The noose is just big enough for the animals head to go through. The unsuspecting animal runs through the loop and sets off the trigger, springing the spring pole which causes the loop to tighten around the animal's neck, choking him. It does not sling him into the air, breaking his neck as some think.*

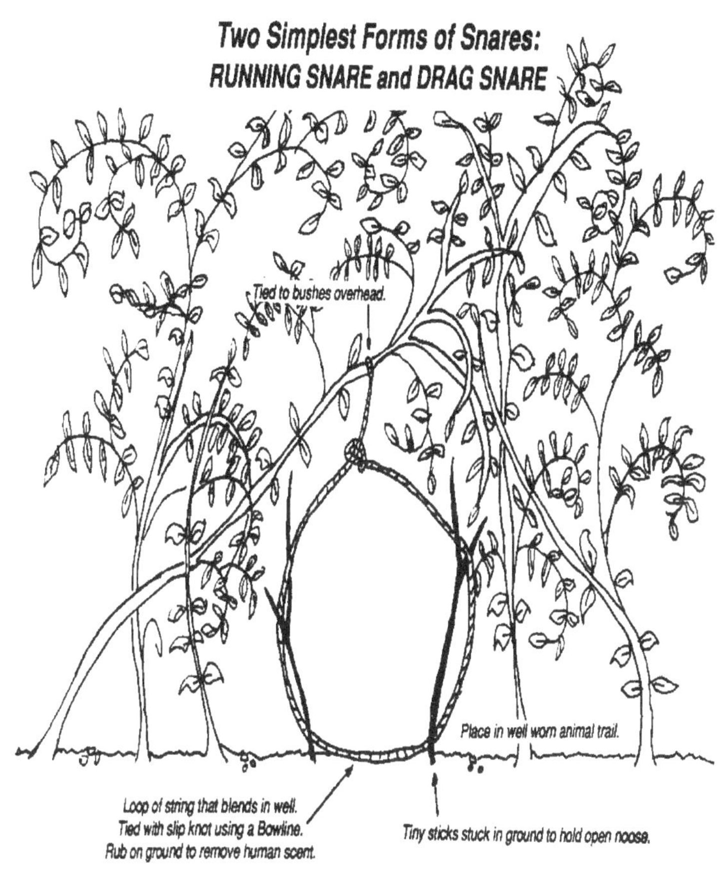

Drag Snare is set up same as Running Snare, except it is used when there is no branches overhead to tie noose to. Instead noose is tied to a bundle of sticks. As animal drags sticks the noose is tightened around its neck.

SHELTER

Lean-To

The lean-to is a good choice if constructed properly. I like to construct a double lean-to or some type of reflector wall in front of my lean-to for the purpose of reflecting heat into the area where I will be sleeping (see pictures and drawing). You then build a trench fire the entire width of the opening and lay across the width parallel to the fire. This will maximize warmth from your fire. In case of a double lean-to one party sleeps in one lean-to and another party sleeps in the other with fire between the two lean-to's with both parties benefiting from the fire.

Lean-to Framework

Double Lean-To. One Not Covered.

Completed Lean-to with framework of another lean-to facing. You may build side walls also if you prefer.

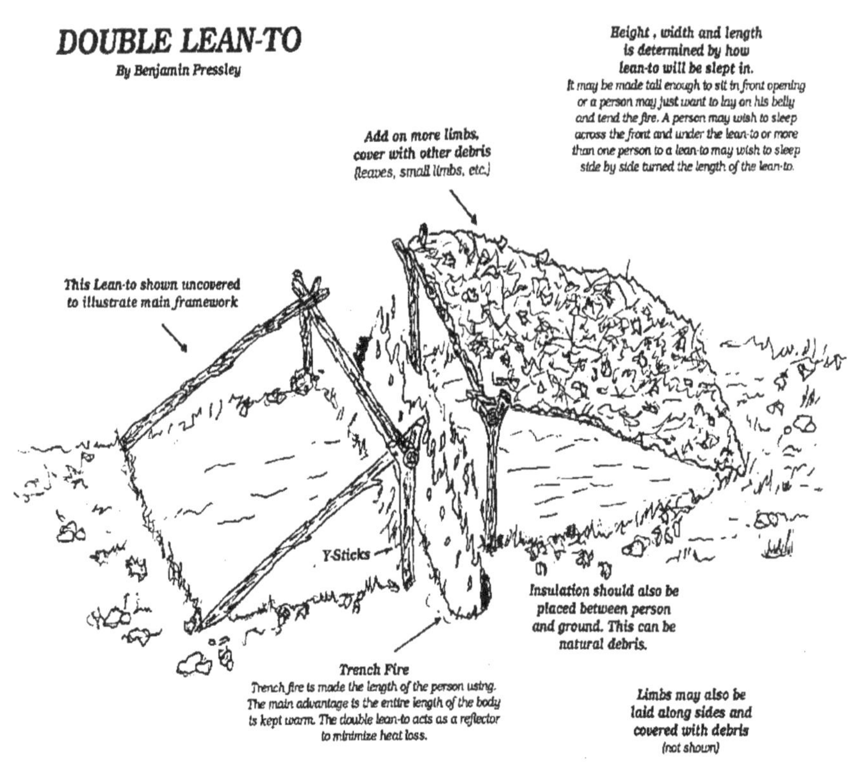

There are many possibilities for shelter. Space does not permit me here to cover the bark covered shelter, the cattail leaf covered shelter and many others. Again, be resourceful. Work with what you have.

Ground Beds

Ground beds are generally of two different types. One is a debris bed and the other is a hot coal bed. Ground beds are only practical if you are in an area where it is safe to sleep on the ground. Concerns would be particularly aggressive insects or known predators that could harm you in your sleep. In cases such as these you need to get up off of the ground and build a platform or hammock of some type.

A debris bed is as simple as enclosing a space with logs and then filling it with soft dry debris such as leaves, pine needles or dried grass. Build the layer of debris 24-36 inches because it will pack down as you sleep on it. Choosing soft, level high ground, if possible, is important also.

A hot coal bed is a little more involved and tricky to sleep on. Basically you dig out a space big enough on the ground that you are going to sleep on and dig a depth of eight inches in the ground. You then build a fire and let coals burn down till you have a good layer of coals. Then you cover the coals with about eight inches of dirt and smooth it out and you lay on top of this space. As the heat of the coals comes through the ground it will heat you and keep you warm. The tricky part is if you are one of those who roll around a lot during your sleep and you dig a spot out accidentally while you're sleeping you will get burned.

This is the framework for a Chickee, a Seminole shelter. It will be layered with thatching on the roof and halfway down sides leaving an opening all the way around the bottom.

FIRE

TYPES OF FIRES

Reflector Fire: A reflector used with a fire allows you to project the heat from flames to a selected spot, more or less. Fire is omnidirectional with most heat travelling upward. A reflector is good for providing warmth to an open shelter. Most cooking is done on coals, however, a reflector allows you to reflect the heat of flames for cooking meat dangling from a tripod or stick or for baking bread and such. One should never cook directly on or in an open flame. Flames are hotter than coals and more difficult to regulate. A reflector can be as simple as logs stacked up and staked on both sides, by a fire or a three-sided reflector can be constructed, thus utilizing even more heat. In a long term camp, mud may even be placed between logs to seal all cracks, but is usually not necessary, provided all knots are removed and logs used are fairly straight.

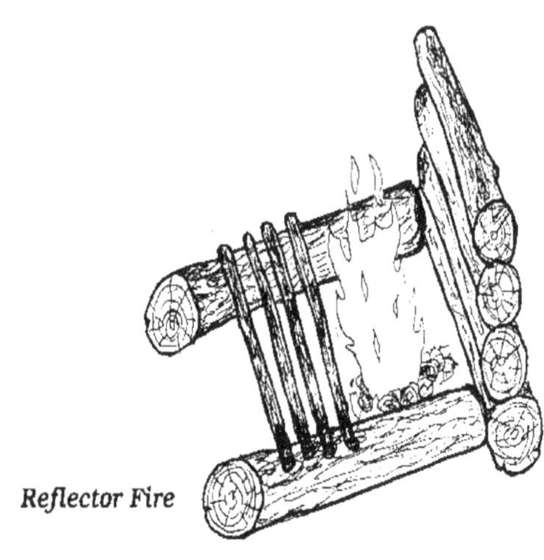
Reflector Fire

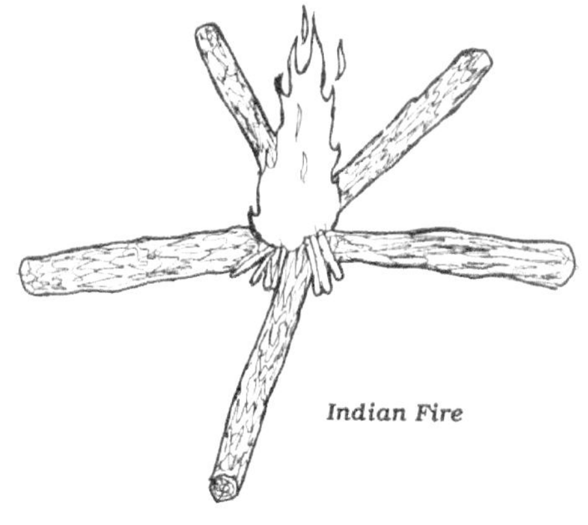

Indian Fire: The Indian fire is a good way to keep you from having to cut up a lot of logs. It also helps preserve fuel when there is not much to be had. Just lay four or five logs down, touching in their centers and radiating outward from the center. Build your tinder and kindling up at the midpoint. As the logs burn, just gradually push them in toward the middle. This works well on long logs that you don't wish to cut or have no means of cutting. In a survival situation you do not want to expend a lot of energy chopping wood. So, why chop wood when it can just burn. Logs can be placed across any fire to burn in half, if your fire is going well enough, rather than chopping them in half. However, split wood does burn easier.

FLINT AND STEEL FIREMAKING

Historical Perspective

The importance of a good fire on the American frontier can hardly be understated. Fire provided warmth in the cold weather and even in the warm weather provided light and was essential for cooking, purifying water and aiding in the manufacture of various useful items just as it is today.

Flint and steel firemaking was probably the most used method of the white settler in the American backcountry, for matches did not appear until the late 19th century and were often unreliable and not readily available. Flint and steel firemaking is still a very simple and reliable method of making fire without matches even today (save some of the modern matchless devices on the market, i.e. magnesium fire starters, a variation of the flint and steel). Success in making fire without matches is achieved only with practice and the right equipment.

The Right Equipment

The essential equipment for flint and steel firemaking, whether acquired or made should be chosen and prepared with care. To the early settler it could be a matter of life and death. To the outdoor survivalist it could still be so. Essential items needed in a flint and steel firemaking kit are as follows:

Fire Steels or Strikers

Fire Steel or Flint Striker

These come in various shapes and sizes, but a broken file works great. The matter of importance here is that it be of high carbon steel. It is always best to test the striker before purchasing it to see if it throws a good shower of orange sparks when properly struck against the flint chard. Yellow sparks indicate a low carbon content and will not be as 'hot'. You can make one easily from a broken file. If using a broken file I have had the best performance from an American made file. They seem to consistently be of a higher carbon content than the cheaper, imported variety. You should also grind the striking edge smooth.

Flint Chard

Black English flint seems to work the best, however, I have had equal success with agate, chert, rhyolite, quartzite or any silica type stone broken into angular chunks to produce sharp edges. A good sharp edge is very important to achieving a good shower of sparks, for it is the flint that is actually shearing off hot particles of steel that produces the sparks necessary for producing a healthy ember.

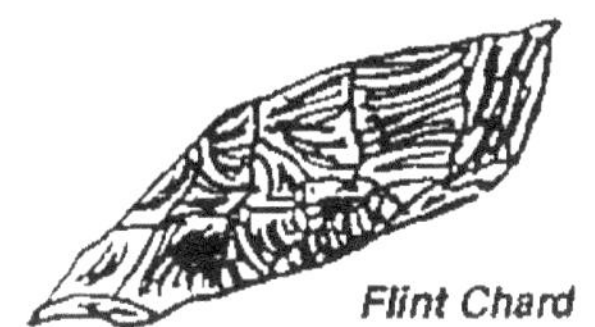
Flint Chard

Charred Cloth

Charred cloth is sometimes referred to as just 'char'. Charred cloth is any natural (cotton, linen, etc.) woven material that is scorched in an airtight container with a hole that allows for the release of gases but not combustion (burning) of the material. There will be more later on producing this all important item as well as a list of raw materials of

Charred Cloth

the wild that can be charred. Once suitable 'char' is produced it should be stored in a tight, waterproof container. A tight, tin container that had been 'japaned' was a common storage place in the backcountry. You can 'japan' your own metal container just by throwing it in a fire and burning off any paint. Then sand it a little to clean it up. I also like rubbing a little oil on it while it is hot, kind of like seasoning a cast iron skillet. A container treated in this manner usually will not rust.

FIRE STEEL or FLINT STRIKER

FOR MAKING FLINT & STEEL FIRES

By Benjamin Pressley

-1993-

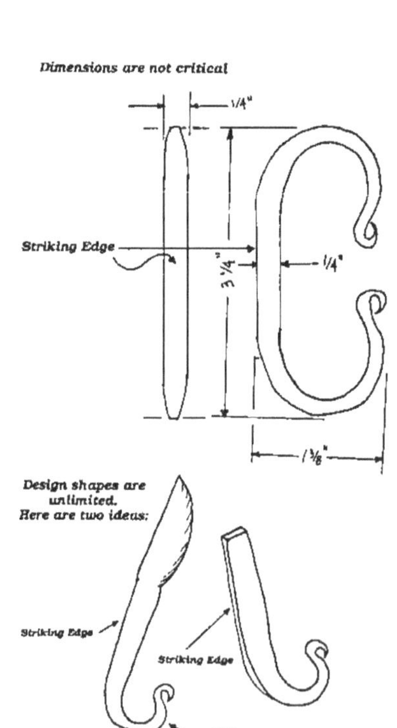

Shape and size are not critical, provided it is comfortable in your hand while using. The design shown to the left is made to to be held while wrapping around your four fingers. Important design considerations is that the striking edge be smooth ground and that the striker be composed of a high carbon steel. This can be tested when struck against a flint chard, or any volcanically produced stone with a sharp edge. it will throw off orange sparks as it scrapes off hot pieces of steel. If it throws off yellow sparks then it is not of a high enough carbon content.

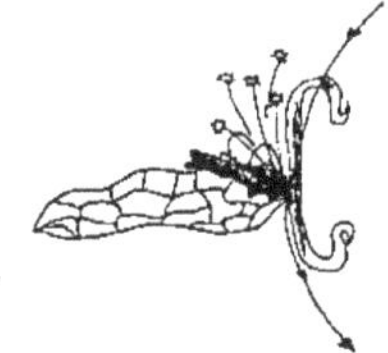

Note the manner of striking the steel against the flint. It is a limp-wristed striking motion, raking across the entire length of the steel, throwing sparks upward to the waiting char cloth on top of the flint chard.

Tinder

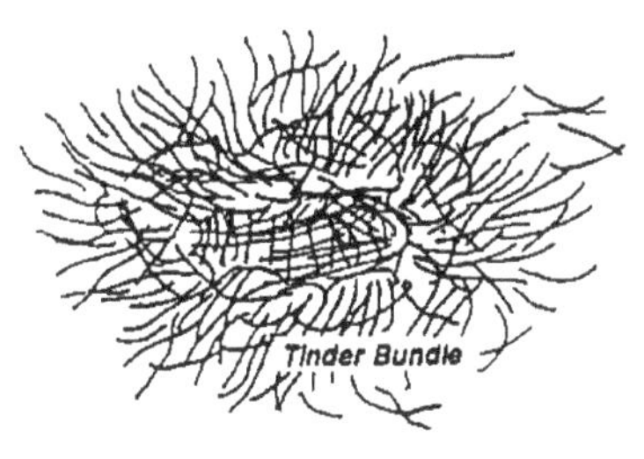

Tinder is any natural material that is easily blown into a flame when an ember is placed in the midst of it. It is also important that this item be kept dry. It can be carried in a leather pouch that contains the other items in your kit if it is constructed in such a way as to be waterproof. Moisture does have a way of penetrating and accumulating though, therefore, it is recommended that some amount of tinder be hermetically sealed in a watertight container. Rivercane or Bamboo that is cut with a section remaining as a bottom and a larger piece for a cap or a wooden plug sealed with beeswax or paraffin serves this purpose well. I know of more than one woodsman that can testify that they were glad they took the time to do this when caught in a downpour or overturned canoe!

Keep your tinder dry. Moisture has a way of penetrating and accumulating though, therefore, it is recommended that some amount of tinder be hermetically sealed in a watertight container.

Here is a list of tinders I have found to be very successful, it is by no means exhaustive, don't be afraid to experiment with others:

- CEDAR BARK (Juniperus occidentalis) - -Peel the stips off of trees that are already loose. Rub it between the hands until it is light and fluffy and all the hard bark is removed leaving nothing but fibers.

- JUTE (Corchorus capsularis) or SISAL (*Agave sisalana)* --You can purchase a roll of jute or sisal fairly inexpensively. Tear it apart into fibers and make a loose tinder nest. Beware though and test your string as a tinder ahead of time because some manufacturers actually treat it with a fire resistant coating.
- MOUSE and BIRD NESTS—Use as is.
- DOGBANE—Dogbane should be worked down to its fibers carefully separating the hardened inner pith and rub between hands till fluffy and soft. This plant is best gathered after the first frost, when it is very dead and dry.
- DRY MOSS—Experiment with this one. Some moss works better than others and some doesn't work at all.

Other Useful But Non-Essential Items

That covers the essentials needed for a good flint and steel firemaking kit. There are other helpful items that may also be included, such as:

- CANDLE STUBS—Birthday candles, any candles. If you use a candle lantern when those candles in your lantern burn down, save them. A candle may be blown into a flame with only an ember from your char and may burn long enough to build moist tinder around until a fire is built. Not to mention that shavings of paraffin or bees wax make a good tinder when all but moist tinder is to be found and can be added to a struggling flame.

- FUZZ STICK—A fuzz stick is good to have. This is just a shaved stick that still has the shavings curled up and clinging to it. This is easily made in the wilderness situation, though, so there is no need to carry one. A pointed end is also helpful for driving into the ground.
- PUNK WOOD—Punk wood is corky, rotten wood. It is a handy item to have, for you can place a piece of glowing 'char' on a piece of it and it will not flame up but will form a larger coal for you to work with the more you blow on it. This is often called a coal enhancer.
- CATTAIL (*Typha* spp. L. (*T. latifolia, T. glauca, T. angustifolia, T. domingensis*)) FLUFF or PLANT DOWN—These are handy to have for 'holding' an ember for a long period of time when you are short on char and candle stubs. These are also coal enhancers.

Making 'Char'

Without a doubt 100% cotton or linen are the best materials for making reliable char. Linen may be laid on a grill over very low coals and blackened, not burned. If it even flames up it becomes a useless ash. It should be removed when it is thoroughly blackened and still holds together well.

The best way to make char though is to acquire a can with a tight fitting lid, such as a paint can, clean it out well and make sure it is thoroughly dry and punch a hole in the lid with a nail. Cut your cotton or linen material to suitable sizes that it will stack and lay flat in the can or cut to the size of your chosen storage container. Place the cloth in the can and put the lid on tightly and set it in the coals and wait. You may wish to put a wire handle on your char can for easy removal later. Black gases will soon begin to escape through the nail hole. This is a good indication that your cloth is charring properly and not burning.

Watch until the gases stop completely, then, remove the can from the heat. Place the nail in the hole loosely or a small stick to prevent any oxygen from entering. Allow to cool before opening the can. This is important, opening it sooner may cause the material to burst into flames and be lost. After it is cool look into the can at your material. If it is black throughout, and not just an ash, then you have been successful. Take some out and strike a spark to it and see how well it holds an ember. If there are any brown areas, then close it up and let it 'cook' a while longer. If you have a material that looks like black plastic or the can is coated with this black plastic, then the material you chose contained some synthetic blend. You might as well throw this away, clean your can out good and look again for some 100% cotton or linen.

A word should be said about natural materials that can be found in the wild that char well. They are charred in the same manner, using a can. One of these is a type of red shelf fungus that grows on the side of oak trees like a shelf. It can be charred and stored whole. Also the cottony pith from many plants ground to a powder and charred works well, these include: Mullein (Verbascum thapsus), Sumac (*Rhus coriaria)*, Elderberry (*Sambucus canadensis)*, etc. In a pinch charcoal from an old fire works and of course, has no need of further charring.

Making 'Char'

Without a doubt 100% cotton or linen are the best materials for making reliable char. Linen may be laid on a grill over very low coals and blackened, not burned. If it even flames up it becomes a useless ash.

Author Benjamin Raven dressed as 18th c. Longhunter

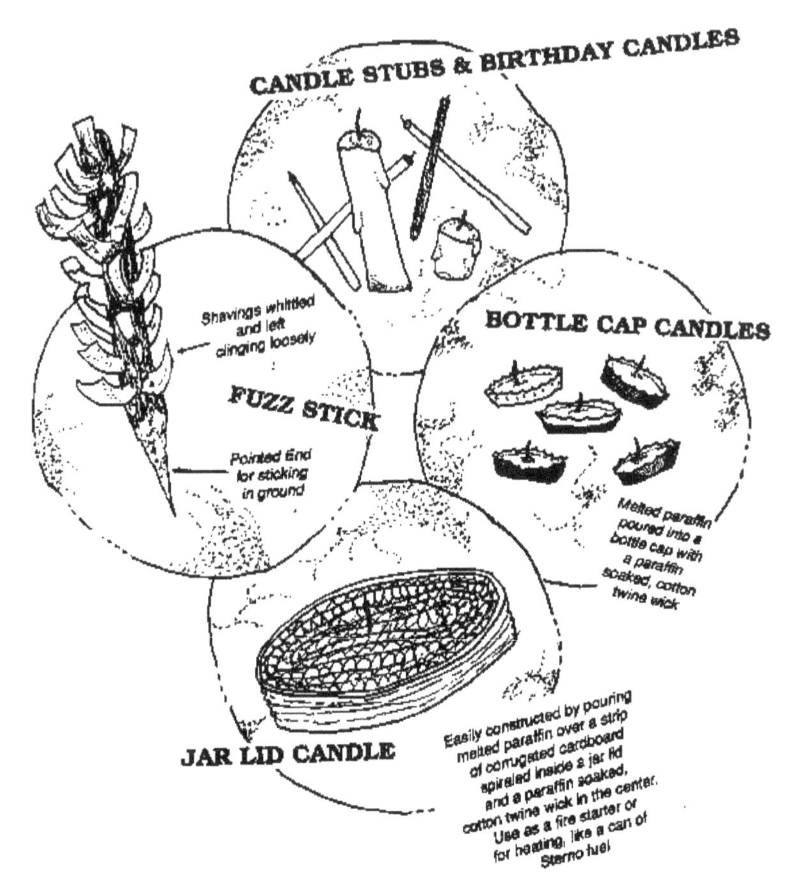

HANDY FIRE STARTERS
Especially Under Wet Conditions

Making Fire With Flint And Steel

Before striking that first spark, go ahead and lay out some small twigs and dry grass and possibly some kindling. Think about what kind of fire you are going to build. It is never necessary to build a bigger fire than needed. If it is a high wind, you may wish to dig a pit. Think ahead. Plan your fire. You don't want your fire to go out while you frantically search for material to keep it going after you get a flame. Next, take out some tinder and form a hollow in the center where it forms a nest of sorts. Lay this aside, but within reach. Tear off a piece of char, you be the judge of how much, usually a piece the size of a quarter is sufficient to blow into a flame in a properly prepared, dry nest of tinder. Place the char on top of your flint chard next to a good sharp edge.

Now, holding the char on the flint with the thumb take your fire steel in your other hand. Strike the flint with the fire steel in a downward, limp-wristed, motion in an arc, not straight up and down, scraping across the length of the fire steel as you go down (see inset on Fire Steel diagram and photo above). You may wish to practice this without char. You will know you are doing it right when you see a nice shower of orange sparks fly. What you are doing is shearing off hot pieces of steel with the flint chard. In one or more attempts you will notice a tiny orange glow in your char. If your char was prepared properly this glow will not go out but will hold until it consumes the material. You may blow on it lightly, if you wish, to get a larger ember. Drop your flint and steel and transfer this glowing char to your tinder nest in the hollow you have prepared. As I said, properly prepared char will not go out, unless moisture has got to it, so you really don't have to blow on it to keep it going until you are ready to blow it into a flame. Now wrap the tinder loosely around the glowing ember. Tilt your head back while holding it slightly above your head and begin to blow on it (See photo). This keeps smoke from filling your eyes and from starting an unplanned brushfire of human hair from the ensuing flame! It will begin to smoke, indicating you are near the tinder's combustion point. Continue blowing steadily until it bursts into flame, then transfer it to your waiting twigs and grass and continue to fuel as normal. You may wish to light a candle at this point to save on char if your flame happens to go out.

That is the best and easiest way. Some prefer to go ahead and lay the char in the tinder nest and then strike flint against steel showering their tinder/char nest on the ground with sparks until it glows and then pick it up and blow it into a flame. It is good to master both, for in the case of powdered char, such as mullein, elderberry and other natural chars discussed earlier you will have to use this method while using the form of the nest to keep the powder together into one mass, as much as is possible.

Another handy thing to master is the art of lighting a candle from the glowing char without benefit of tinder. This is particularly handy when you are out of tinder and nothing can be found. Master it and you may like it so well that you prefer it over carrying tinder. Select a piece of char cloth about 3 inches by 2 inches and roll it end to end creating a tight roll about the diameter of a pencil. Position the roll of char on top of your flint with one end near the sharp edge you are going to strike. As you strike the fire steel on the flint you want to cause the sparks to fall on the end of the roll of charred cloth. When they catch and the cloth is glowing, drop the flint and steel and pick up the candle and place the roll alongside it. Blow long and steady breaths onto the smoldering end of the cloth. Blowing the cloth will cause the cotton or linen you charred to reach it's combustion point but it cannot burst into flame because all the burnable gases have been driven off during the charring process. It will however, melt some of the wax on the side of the candle and absorb some of it. This absorbed wax after a few seconds of blowing will burst into flame. Using the blazing roll of char, you can light the candle. This takes a little practice but is well worth mastering. A variation of this was used right through the Civil War. It was a handy implement which was basically a metal tube that had a cotton rope through it. One end was kept charred. A spark was struck to the charred end of the rope and this was used to either light a candle or light a tinder bundle. The rope was then pulled back in enough to smother the flame. Pretty handy and compact. Weld or solder a little ring on the side of the tube and you could carry it around your neck or attach it to your possibles bag.

That pretty much covers flint and steel firemaking, but by no means covers all its variations and other methods of firemaking used by backcountry folk or their predecessors. They did use other firemaking methods, such as fire by friction. The backwoodsman sometimes placed the char in the pan of his rifle and 'lit' the char with the shower of sparks created by flint striking frizzen. In many colonial homes a variation of this was found in a mantlepiece that consisted basically of a gun lock and pan to hold the char. Firemaking is an art almost as old as man and though refined in modern methods still remains one of man's most essential skills.

HUNTING WEAPONS

Blowgun

The blowgun is another weapon that can be produced in the survival situation and is used for hunting small game, such as squirrels. However, I have read accounts of Cherokee boys being so accurate that they would shoot a dart at a deer's eyes blinding them which slowed them enough for them to catch up with them and kill them with their knives.

The blowgun can be made from a pithy centered branch that is split and hollowed out, such as Sumac, like the Houma did, or it is most easily made from a length of River Cane, like the Cherokee. You can also use Bamboo, but the thick sections of bamboo are harder to get out. A good length is ½ to 1 inch in diameter and 4 to 8 feet long. The River Cane blank should first be heat straightened as described earlier for the atlatl darts.

The interior wall joints must be removed. In the survival situation this is best accomplished by splitting the blank into two equal halves down the length of it and using stone flakes or grinding stones to grind them away smoothly. The two halves should then be glued back together with hide glue or pitch glue and bound with buckskin, rawhide or cordage. If you make one at home, you may wish to use a heated steel rod to burn out the sections, instead of splitting the cane and sanding the interior smoothly. Check the straightness once you have all the sections knocked out by looking down the bore. You should be able to see a circle when looking into the light. It is more important to be straight down the bore, even if the outside appears to be crooked. Sometimes if you roll the blowgun in a circle you may find that you see a perfect circle. When you find that point you should mark the top of the blowgun so you know where to turn it when firing a dart. I like to go ahead and tie a light weight string with a fluffy feather on the underside at the other end. That way I know where to turn the blowgun for firing and I have a wind direction indicator built in. I do like Rivercane (*Arundinaria gigantea*) best. River Cane is native to North America, Bamboo (There are 91 genera and about 1,000 species of bamboo. They are all members of the true grass family *Poaceae*, subfamily *Bambusoideae*, tribe *Bambuseae*.) is its Asian cousin. River Cane is much easier to work with than Bamboo. The joints in Bamboo are thicker and can never seemingly be sanded smooth enough. A smooth bore is essential to a blowgun. There should be no left over material inside or anything to slow the exiting dart down. Because of the way plants grow the root end will be a slightly larger diameter than the other. The dart is placed in the larger end and exits the smaller end. This has a 'choke' effect on the dart causing its fletchings to really lay down and a lot of force is built up for the fastest exit possible.

The darts are made by using any lightweight, small diameter wood. Splits of River Cane or Bamboo work well. At home, just for target practice, using Bamboo skewers that you can purchase at your grocer works very well. I use thick walled Cane or Bamboo when I make darts from this material, so it can be rounded. Flat pieces of cane have a tendency to 'plane'. The Cherokee used to overcome this problem by heating the shaft material and twisting it into a corkscrew. The corkscrew design does not make it spin as some have theorized it only stabilizes it by keeping it from planing. For most hunting, though, you will need a heavier shaft material. I prefer split, round diameter, straight-grained hardwood. I like Locust (*Gleditsia triancanthos*) best. Darts should be sharpened on one end and about 10 inches in length. Grind the point, rather than whittling it. It makes for a stronger, longer lasting tip. You also want to really taper the point back, if you don't it acts like a blunt tip and doesn't get the penetration you need. I have seen darts bounce off of squirrel hides before for this very reason. Another alternative that you probably will really find not necessary is to make a tiny point of stone or bone and hafting it in the point end of the dart.

Fletchings should cover about 4 inches of the butt end and can be made from rabbit fur, cotton, Bull thistle (Cirsium vulgare) down, small bird feathers and *some* other plant downs. When choosing fletching

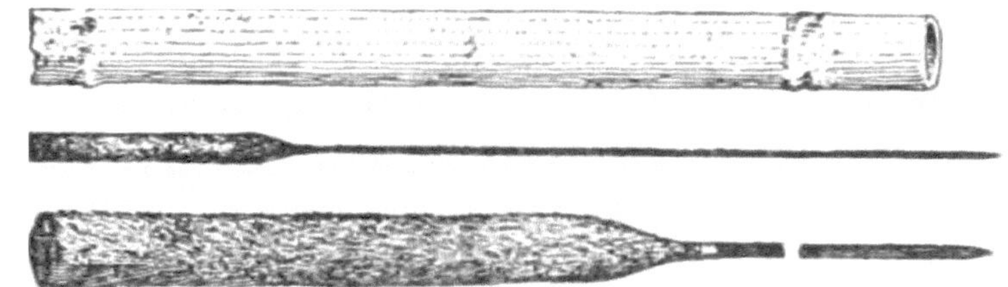

Historic Drawing Showing End Of Blowgun and Thistle Down Fletched Darts As Used By Cherokee.

River Cane Blowgun, Gourd Neck Sheath Containing Darts, Cotton Fletched Dart, Thistle Down Fletched Dart

material, keep in mind: a) The material must be just light enough to give drag to the dart to stabilize it but not outweigh the rest of the dart; and, b) It must also be light and fluffy enough to fill the chamber of your blowgun as air is pushed through from your breath, causing it to be propelled out and yet be able to lay down aerodynamically when exiting the blowgun. Small bird feathers work well, 'fluffs' or very tiny feathers, not stiff spined feathers. I really like small turkey breast and thigh feathers. Tiny feathers must be tied in, layering one row on another as described with thistle down below. Fluffs may sometimes just be tied at the top at a point a few inches from the butt end. I have found fluffs to cause more drag and slow the dart down though. If you use rabbit fur cut a thin strip and spiral wrap it, securing both ends. Rabbit fur is very heavy for a dart, so you will have to experiment with the weight ratio. Cotton can be secured well enough for a one shot dart by just licking the shaft of the dart and rolling it on without string, kind of like the South American aborigine does with the plant down they use called kapok (*Ceiba pentandra*). You can experiment with other downs used in this manner. Cotton works this way because of its long fibers that can be spiral wrapped around the dart, unlike Cattail down that does *not* work. As far as plant downs go, you will have to be very selective. Remember the purpose of the down is to carry the seed of the plant, so you will have to remove the heavy seeds and they will have to be secured in the same manner as described next with the thistle down. *It cannot just be rolled in glue!* Which brings us to Thistle down. Thistle down is the material of choice. Get a bulb that is dried but not opened or catch them before they open and tie them shut and allow them to dry till you're ready to use them. Native Americans would split a piece of cane and clamp bulbs between the two halves tied together until they were ready to use. Remove the down carefully, keeping it flat and in one line. Carefully remove the seeds, brown chaff and rough up and soften the hard areas that held the seed, while keeping tightly clamped between your thumb and forefinger. Holding a length of cordage in your mouth, with the other end secured in a notch in the butt end of the shaft of the dart you are rolling, so one hand holds the dart shaft, while the other holds the thistle down. Secure the fletching material by wrapping it with the cordage catching just enough of an edge to hold it and allow it to fluff out as you move down the entire fletching area, feeding the down into the string as you go and tie off at the end.

The dart should slide in the blowgun easily but snug. It is placed in the end you will blow, flush, point first. You may even want to insert the freshly made dart to the depth you want it and burn the excess while in the blowgun making a nice flat finish. The blowgun is held with both hands with the elbows resting on the chest and together. The dart is then blown with a sudden burst of air after aiming at the target.

The blowgun is used in many cultures throughout the world. You will be impressed with the accuracy and distance you can achieve with it with very little practice. Everyone has seen the *National Geographic* specials with the South American aborigine bringing down monkeys with a poisoned dart with a blowgun ten feet long or more. They often used poison from the mucus of the poison dart frog. If you wish to experiment with some poisons concentrated tobacco works well. Poison is not necessary, however, for most small game and as far as we know was not used in North America. Monkeys have a more advanced nervous system and the additional reassurance of the poison is necessary for hunting them. Most darts are constructed heavy and long enough to bring down most small game.

COMBATIVES

SAFETY IN TRAINING

It cannot be overemphasized that safety should be the paramount consideration during any training activity. That is why this section is repeated in each volume.

SAFETY REMINDER

We train so that we can protect ourselves and not get hurt. Why then would we allow being hurt in training? It is the responsibility of the instructor and all class participants to ensure the safety of all. All participants in a training activity should be led through a proper warm up and stretching routine before class begins.

SAFETY EQUIPMENT

Scouts should also use appropriate safety equipment for all training sessions. Equipment that should be used includes:

- -Athletic Cup
- -Athletic Mouth Piece
- -Safety head gear
- -Forearm shields
- -Safety Goggles
- -Safety Gloves

SAFETY TRAINING WEAPONS

Scouts should also use safe training weapons. A variety of training blades should be used from rubber to aluminum trainers. Dulled Live blades are inappropriate for anything but solo training purposes. NO LIVE WEAPONS SHOULD EVER BE ALLOWED IN THE TRAINING AREA. A good friend of mine was working in a seminar with another instructor. The Instructor drew his blade and cut my friend across the inside of his forearm as part of his demo. The only problem is that he drew his live blade and not a trainer. Luckily a few stitches were all that were needed that day. I shudder to think what would have happened if the instructor would have been demonstrating a neck cut.

OTHER CONSIDERATIONS

- Training should be conducted in reasonable proximity of emergency medical care
- Training should be conducted in a designated training area with adequate flooring, padding and ventilation.

SAMPLE FORCE CONTINUUM

ATTACKER'S ACTION	YOUR RESPONSE
Cooperation	**Verbal Commands**
Passive Resistance	**Escort Control**
Active Resistance	**Control & Compliance Holds**
Assault Which Can Result in Bodily Harm	**Defensive Tactics/Mechanical Controls/Less Lethal Weapons**
Assault Which Can Result In Serious Bodily Harm or Death	**Deadly Force**

**The use of force continuum presented is a general model based on common U.S. use of force guidelines. The continuum presented is for illustrative purposes only. The reader is responsible for following all local, state and federal laws.*

USE OF FORCE

It cannot be overemphasized that understanding of the use of force and how it should be used during any training activity and in real life application. That is why this section is repeated in each volume.

Force Continuum

The force continuum is a conceptual tool which exists to aid in determining what level of force is required and justified in controlling the actions of an attacker. Verbal commands, escort techniques, mechanical controls, and deadly force are all options which are available to a person depending upon the attacker's actions. Force escalation must cease when the attacker complies with the commands of the individual, and/or the situation is controlled by the individual. The model presented bellow consists of five levels. Physical defensive tactics are appropriate from levels three to five.

- **Level One:** The attacker cooperates with your verbal commands. Physical actions are not required.
- **Level Two:** The attacker is unresponsive to verbal commands. Attacker cooperation however is achieved with escort techniques.
- **Level Three:** The attacker actively resists your attempts to control without being assault. Compliance and control holds as well as pain compliance techniques are appropriate actions at this time.
- **Level Four:** The attacker assaults you or another person with actions which are likely to

cause bodily harm. Appropriate action would include mechanical controls or defensive tactics such as stunningtechniques. Impact and chemical weapons may be appropriate at this level.

- **Level Five:** The attacker assaults you or another person with actions which are likely to cause serious bodily harm or death if not stopped immediately. Appropriate action could include deadly force through mechanical controls, Impact weapons or firearms. Deadly force should be considered only when all avenues for escape have been exhausted, as well as when lesser means have been exhausted, are unavailable or cannot be reasonably employed.

DECISION OF FORCE

When making the decision to use force you should use the minimal amount of "Reasonable" force necessary to safely control the situation at hand. When using deadly force for self defense you must be prepared to articulate and justify their use of a force.

"Reasonable force" can be defined: *force that is not excessive and is the least amount of force that will permit safe control of the situation while still maintaining a level of safety for himself or herself and the public"* You may be justified in the use of force when they reasonably believe it to be necessary to defend yourself or another from bodily harm and have no avenue for reasonable escape. Escalation and de-escalation of resistance and response may occur without going through each successive level. You have the option to escalate or disengage, repeat the technique, or escalate to any level at any time. However, you will need to justify any response to resistance.

TOTALITY OF CIRCUMSTANCES

Totality of circumstances refers to all facts and circumstances known to you at the time. The totality of circumstances includes consideration of the attacker's form of resistance, all reasonably perceived factors that may have an effect on the situation, and the response options available to you.

SAMPLE FACTORS MAY INCLUDE THE FOLLOWING:

- Severity of the assault or battery
- Attacker is an immediate threat
- Attacker's mental or psychiatric history, if known to you
- Attacker's violent history, if known to you
- Attacker's combative skills
- Attacker's access to weapons
- Innocent bystanders who could bc harmed
- Number of attacker's you are facing
- Duration of confrontation
- Attacker's size, age, weight, and physical condition
- Your size, age, weight, physical condition, and defensive tactics expertise
- Environmental factors, such as physical terrain, weather conditions, etc.

THE COMBAT CLINCH

The Combat Clinch

In this installment we will be taking a look at the combat clinch, and a series of 3 simple and effective techniques that the reader can add to their tool box..

In my experience two individuals find themselves in a clinch under the following circumstances:

- The trained fighter applies a clinch in order to set up an attack.
- An untrained fighter becomes, tired.
- An Untrained fighter becomes frustrated that they are repeatedly being hit, and clinch in an effort to stop the striking action.

Regardless of how you end up in a clinch, your answer to it for realistic self-defense scenarios should be swift, aggressive and decisive. A clinch is a very dangerous position in which to find oneself. You should always seek to fight your way out of the clinch into a position of advantage. Remember not to turn a clinch situation into a wrestling match. Rough and ready is the order of the day.

The clinch solutions presented below are modified from combat sports such as Greco Roman wrestling. The techniques presented illustrate the proper modifications needed to make combat sports functional for real world self-defense.

NECK CLINCH DEFENSE

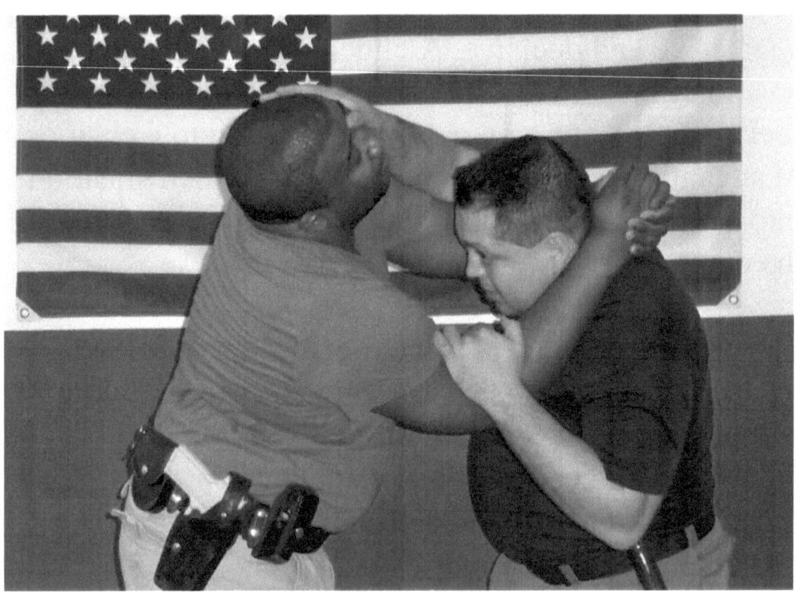

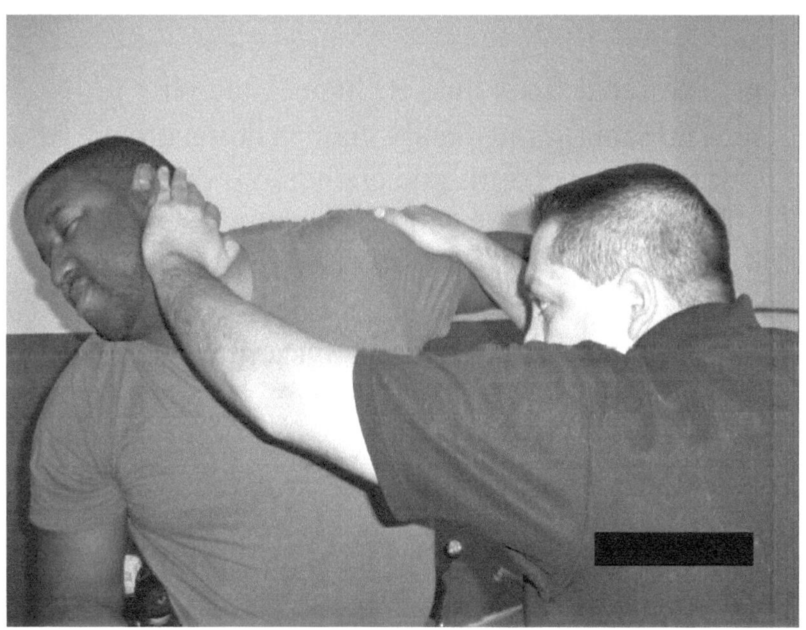

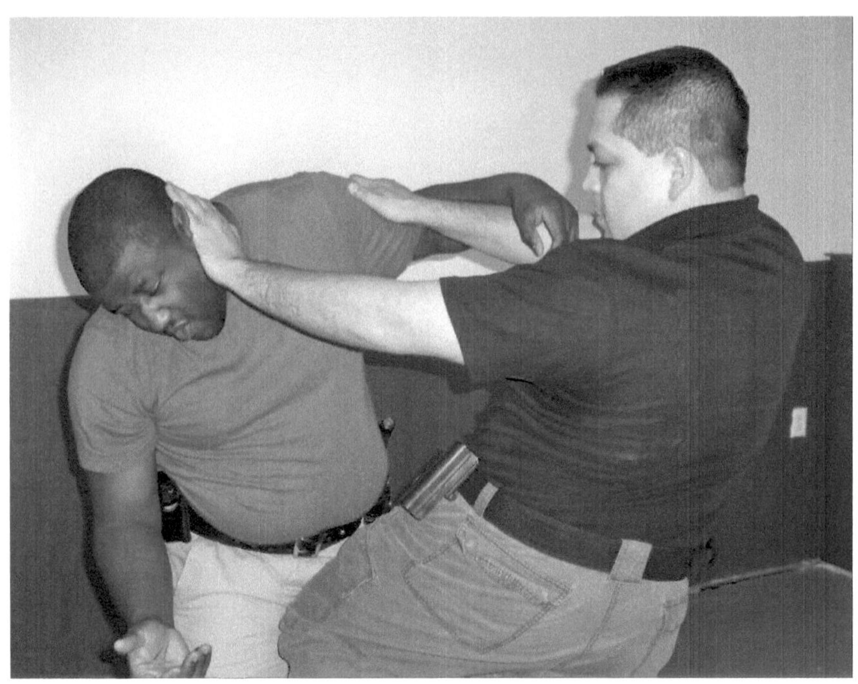

- The scout finds himself in neck clinch.
- The scout immediately clamps down on one of the attackers arms and anchors his own elbow to his side, in effect canting the attacker.
- The scout then drives the opposite arm upwards to the attackers face delivering a eye gouge forcing the attackers head into the direction of the clamped arm.
- The scout then extends his other arm under the extended arm which is attacking the eye. The other arm fans away and takes control of the attackers jaw, forcing him backwards.
- The scout then secures the attackers other arm and executes a knee strike to the attacker.

COLLAR & ELBOW CLINCH DEFENSE

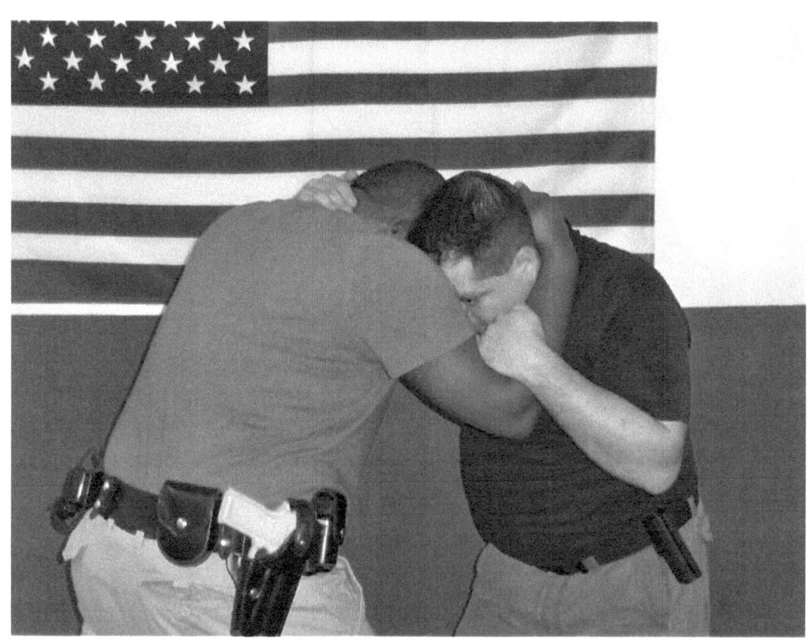

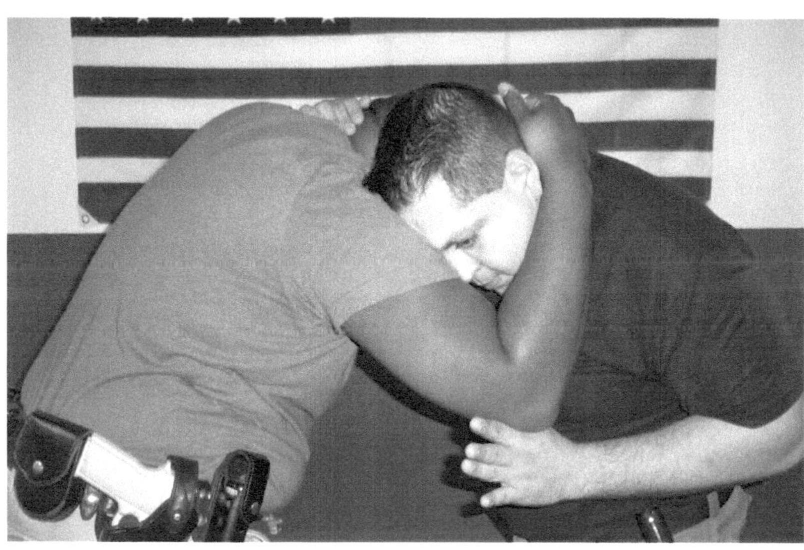

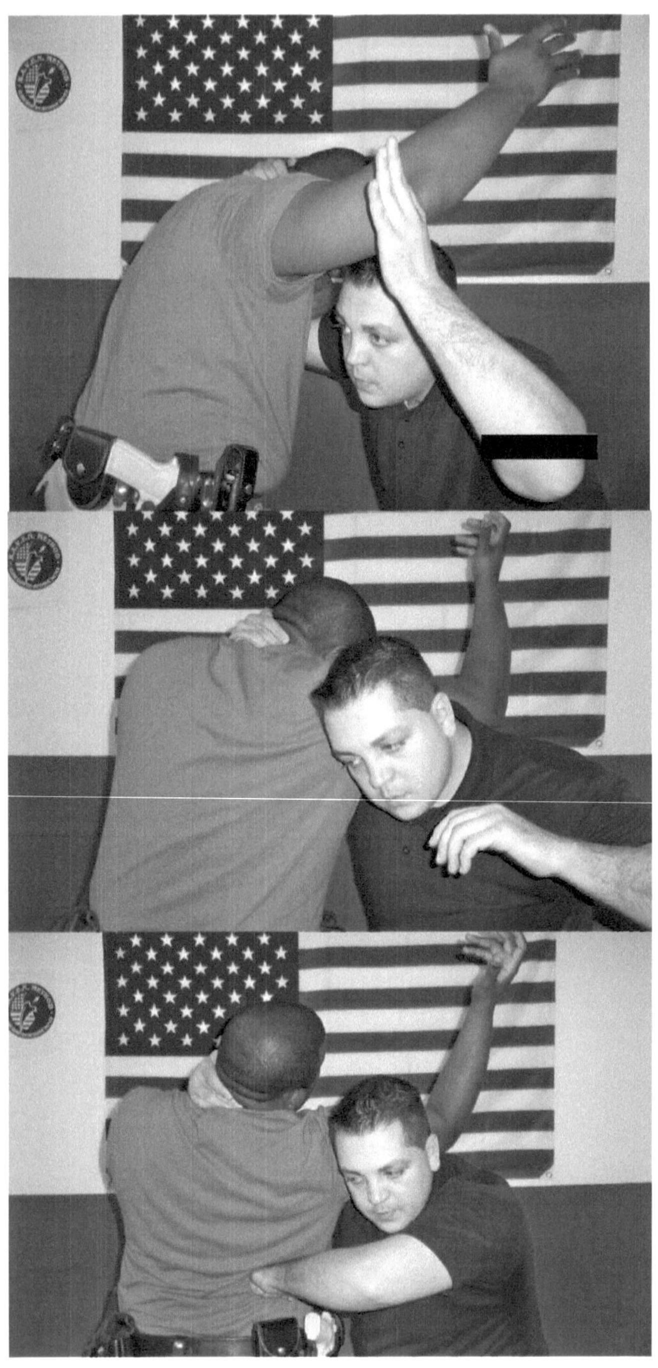

- The scout finds himself in a collar & elbow clinch.
- The scout places his hand under the attackers elbow.
- The scout then simultaneously lifts the elbow up while ducking under the attackers arm and driving forward.
- The scout then tucks his head close to the attacker while pulling down on the attackers neck.
- The scout now delivers a hard blow to the attackers floating rib or kidney area. This blow will help to bring the attackers hips forward taking him out of balance.
- The scout then secures a good grip around the attackers neck, and drives forward while stepping behind the attacker, blocking off his leg to take the attacker down

BODY CLINCH DEFENSE

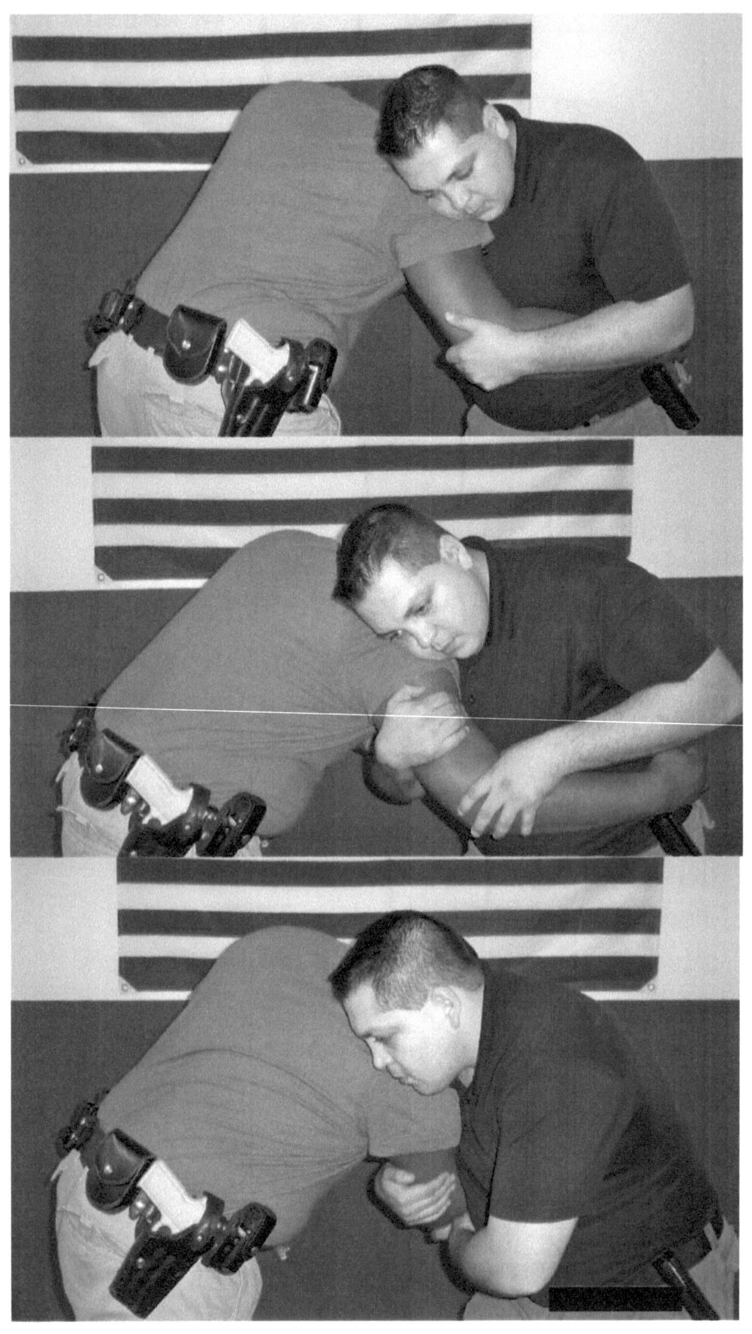

- The scout finds himself in a body clinch
- The scout immediately reaches across his body to the attackers arm, securing an under and over hook
- The scout places his hand on top of the attackers elbow pit and forced the arm down.
- The scout then pushes the attackers arm to the other side of his body, spinning him away from the scout.
- The Scout now shoots his right arm high across the attackers collar bone, and shoots his left hand to the swell of the back of the attacker.
- The scout then steps forward blocking off the attackers legs and simultaneously drives his hands in opposite directions effectively taking down the attacker.

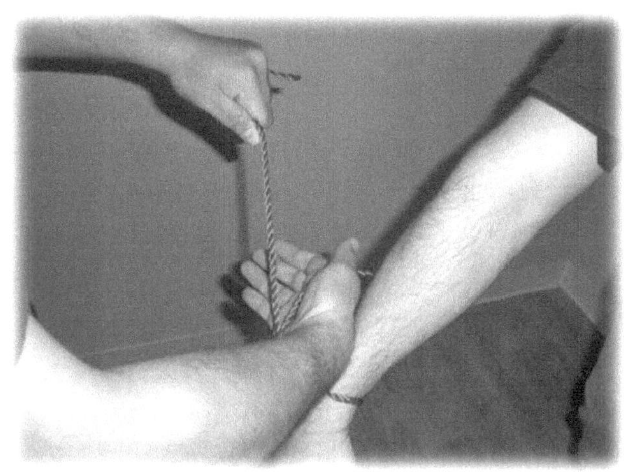

FLEXIBLE WEAPONS

For the purposes of self-defense, an individual should always seek the tactical advantage. Part of attaining this advantage is acquisition and use of weapons to protect oneself. Unfortunately for civilians carrying weapons on ones person can be restricted if not outright illegal. A flexible weapon can be carried into a court room, on an airplane, anywhere you go it goes and the beautiful part about it is that NOBODY ever identifies it as a weapon, so it is there inconspicuous until the moment you need it.

A "FLEX" is usually not a weapon by design, so the issues of perception to the police and a court of law will usually tilt in your favor. Take a knife for example, even an honest person who legally defends themselves with a knife will have to deal with the negative perception associated with knives. Will the jury look at them as some Knife carrying nut who must have had it on him because he was looking for trouble? Now ask yourself if the perception would be as negative if you defended yourself with handkerchief? Chances are pretty good you wouldn't come across as someone "looking for trouble". The "FLEX" is a great self defense weapon which is inexpensive, low key and always accessible. Anyone interested in their own safety should take the time to learn how to use a "FLEX" safely and properly. To get your training started here are a few techniques against a looping punch to include in your tool box. In a wilderness environment, a bandana, or a piece of cordage makes a great flexible weapon.

PROPER GRIP

The proper grip on the weapon for the series of techniques below is right hand palm up and left hand palm down.

UNIVERSAL ENTRY

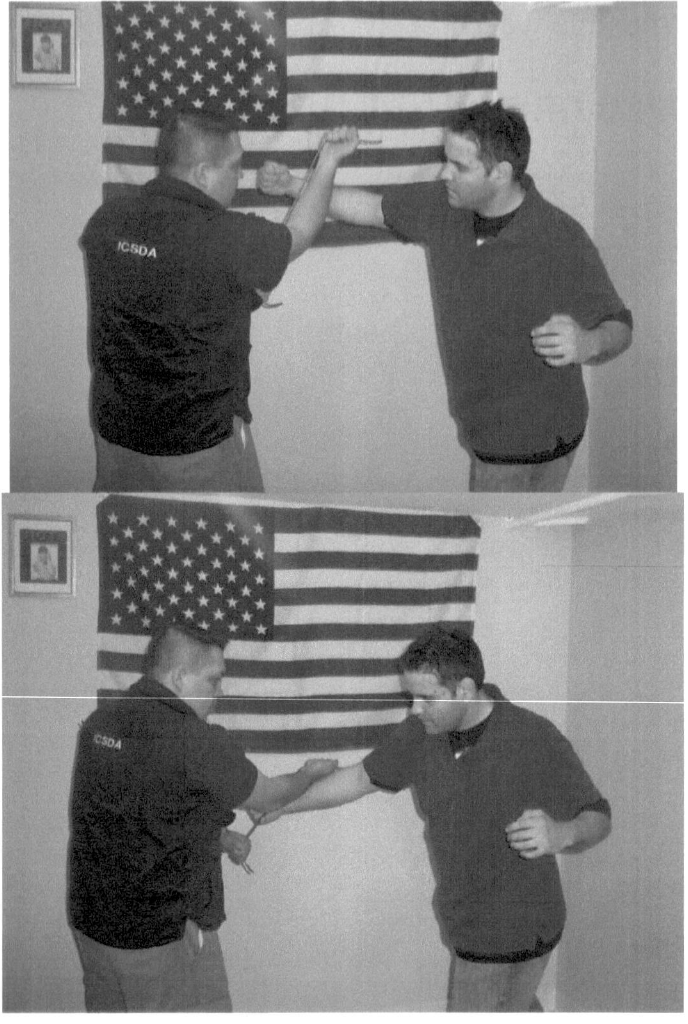

When The attacker launches the looping punch you should block with your forearm allowing the flex to run perpendicular to your arm (do not block with the flex alone).
Once you make contact with the attackers arm start to “pass” the arm downwards and redirect it to your right side.

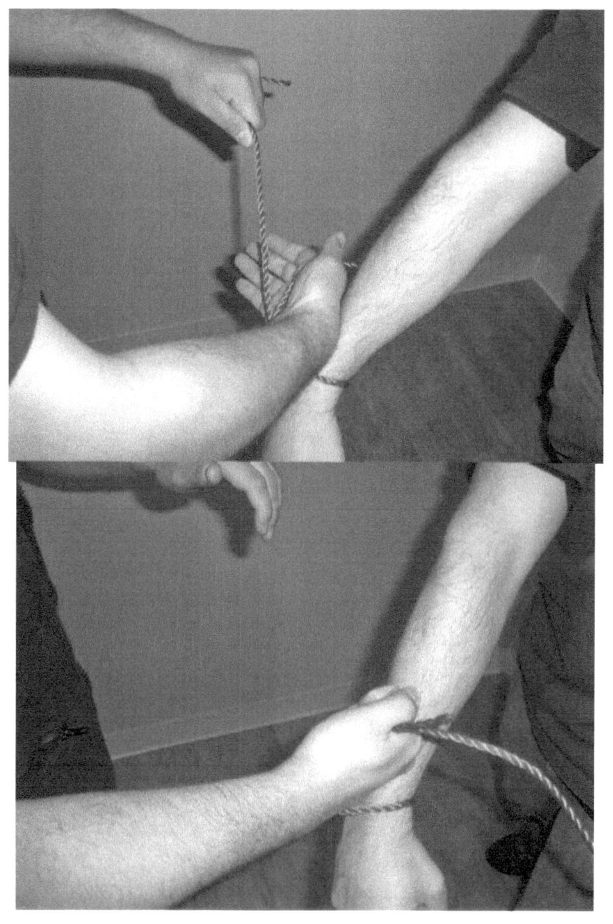

As your right hand comes downwards open your hand slightly and grip the other end of the FLEX.
Now you should have a firm loop around the attackers wrist gripping it with just your right hand.

This is the universal entry for the three techniques that follow. It may seem awkward at first but you will feel comfortable after just a few repetitions. Make sure that you learn this entry well, as the techniques all depend greatly on this initial motion.

TECHNIQUE NUMBER ONE

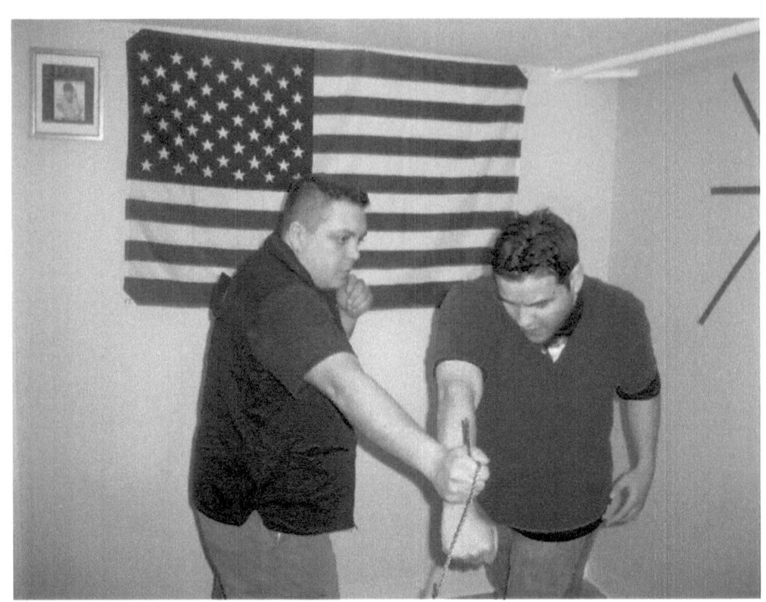

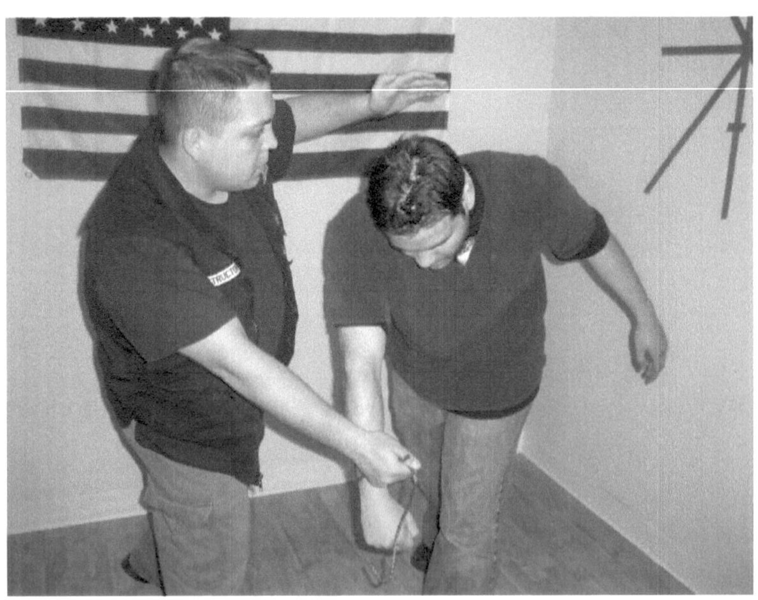

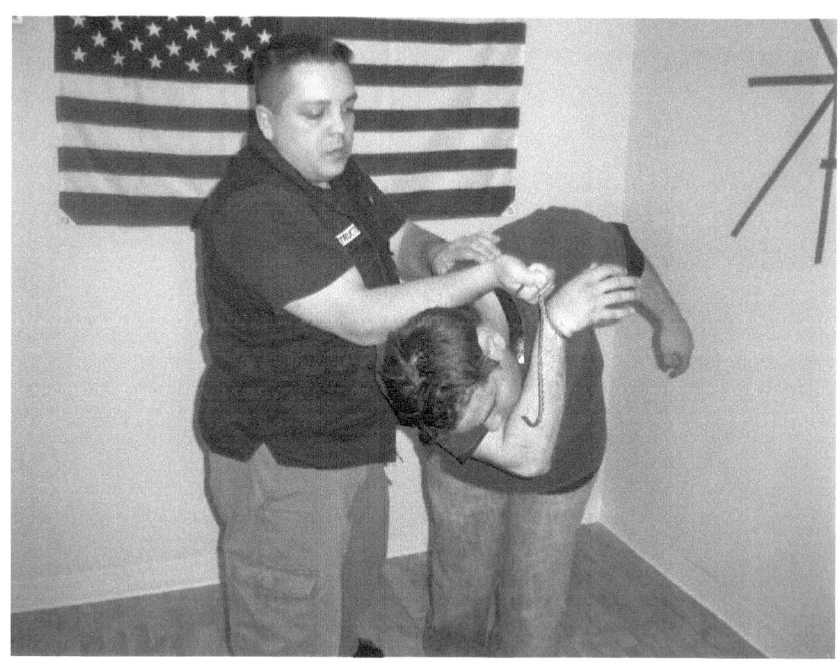

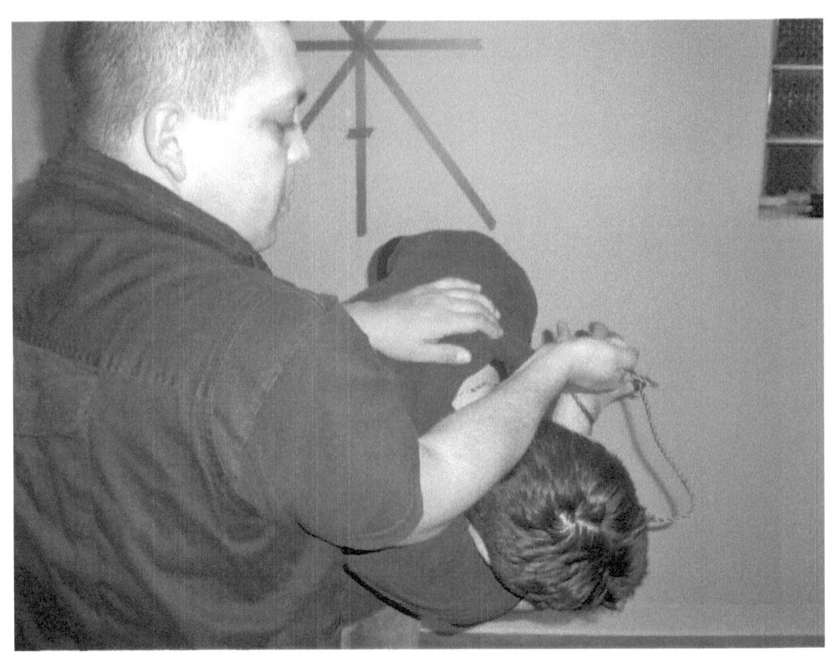

Complete the Universal Entry

- Use your right hand and forcefully jerk the attacker to the right taking him off balance.
- Forcefully Slap the attacker on the back of the neck/base of the skull to get him lowered and moving foreword.
- Control the attacker forward and raise your elbow, push the attackers head under your right arm.
- Place the outside of your forearm on the back of the attackers
- Pull your right arm back and bring your elbow to your center. This will pull the attacker off balance and synch in your hold on him.
- Once the attacker is secured punch your forearm into him and pull your right hand back to keep him off balance.
- Using his elbow as a lever pull the attacker back and off balance. At this point you can let him drop or control him down keeping him "tied up" until help arrives or you make an escape.

TECHNIQUE TWO

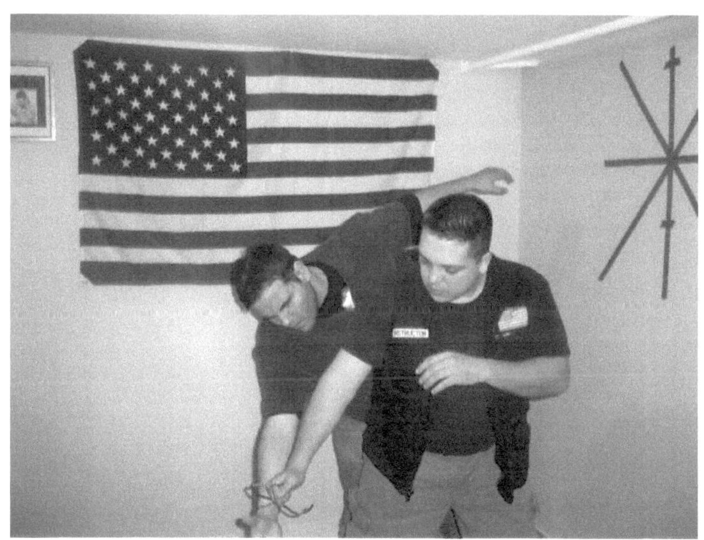

Complete the Universal Entry

- Use your right hand and forcefully jerk the attacker to the right taking him off balance.
- Elevate your right hand bringing the attackers arm up high.
- Step under the attackers arm and through.
- Rapidly pull Your Arm Down.
- Forcefully pull your arm to your left hip, whipping the attacker around.
- Complete your take down
- Once the attacker is down, pull up on his arm to keep him off balance while you assess the situation and wither escape or control him until help arrives.

TECHNIQUE THREE

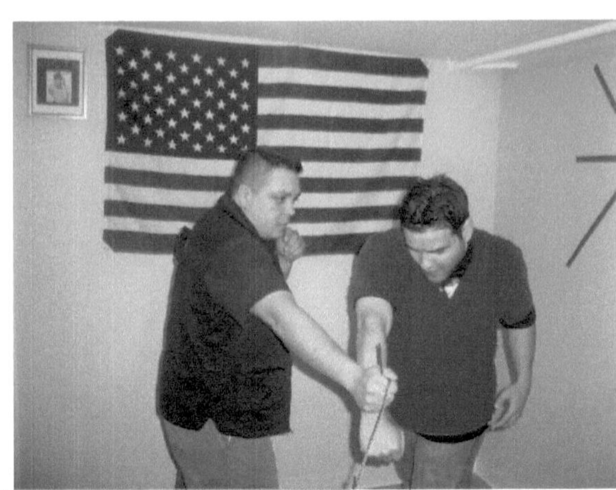

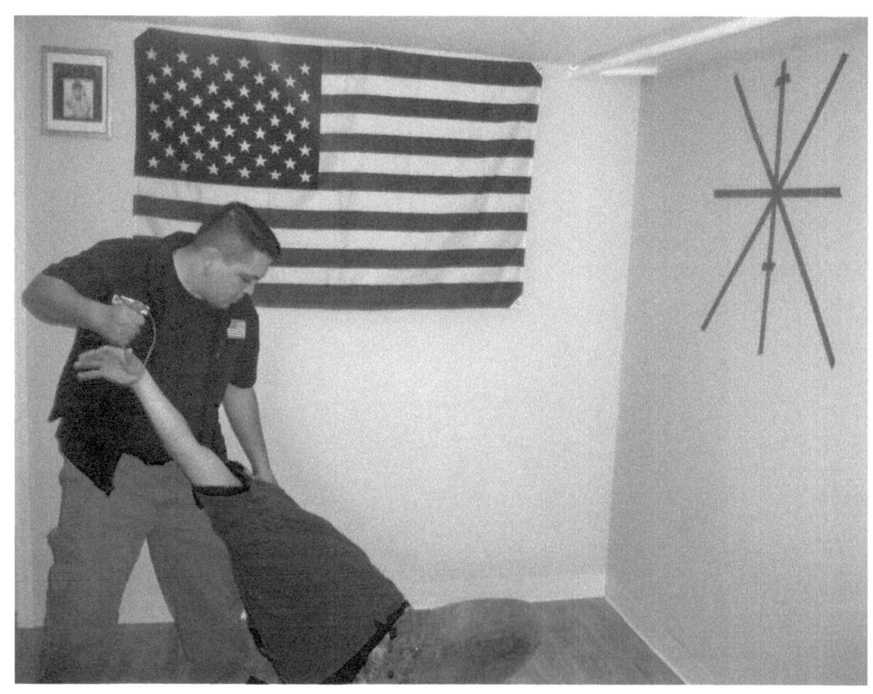

Complete the Universal Entry

- Use your right hand and forcefully jerk the attacker to the right taking him off balance.
- Shoot your left hand into the attackers face, striking with your palm and turning his head away from you. By turning his head away you disrupt his balance.
- pull your left hand in a circular motion to your left hip. This will effect the takedown.
- Once the attacker is down, pull up on his arm to keep him off balance while you assess the situation and wither escape or control him until help arrives.

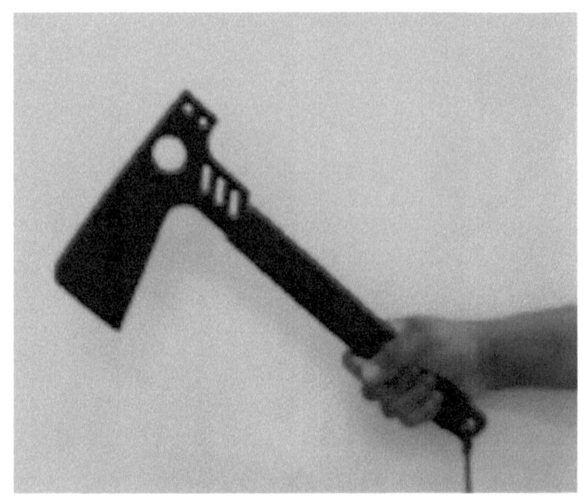

TOMAHAWK

MAKING AND HAFTING A STONE AXE

By Benjamin Pressley

--1992--

Choose a dense glass-like or near glass-like stone, such as Greenstone, Flint or Obsidian...Break it down to a workable size ...Use Direct Percussion methods to reduce it...Use Pecking methods to break out a notch around its middle, if you are going to use a wrapping method of hafting...Grind down edge on an abrasive stone...Until you get something shaped like this:

Un-notched. Haft by forcing into a prepared hole.

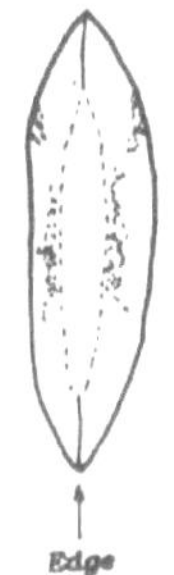

Proper Angle For Edge
...too thin will break too easily. ...too abrupt will not cut well.

Edge

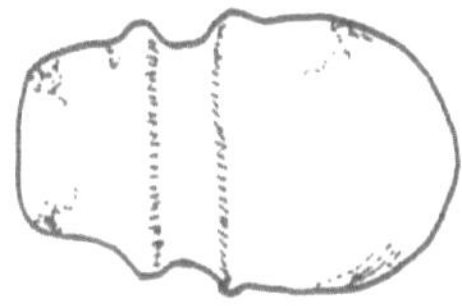

Notched by Pecking. Wrap to haft.

Hafting:

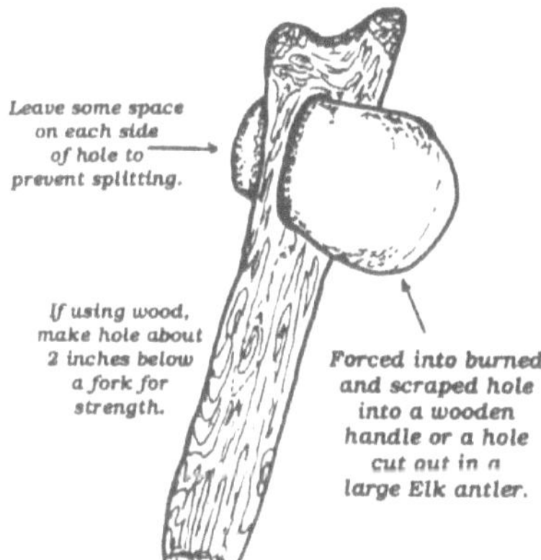

Leave some space on each side of hole to prevent splitting.

If using wood, make hole about 2 inches below a fork for strength.

Forced into burned and scraped hole into a wooden handle or a hole cut out in a large Elk antler.

Green branches from trees, such as Willow may be heated or boiled, if necessary, to aid in bending them around axe. Wrap it twice and bind it tightly with some sturdy cordage.

(Shown loosely wrapped for clarity.)

The axe is one of the earliest tools and weapons formed by man. Primitive axes can be traced back as far as the Stone Age. The axe is a primal tool linked to man's earliest existence. The tomahawk is just one such tool in this family of weapons which can be found in virtually every culture thought history and the world. The tomahawk was an indigenous weapon found in the Americas before European colonization.

The word "tomahawk" is derived from the Algonquian words Tomahak or Tamahakan meaning "used for cutting". Early tomahawks were made with stone heads, which quickly evolved to metal after the Europeans brought new materials and technology to the Americas.

As a weapon the tomahawk was used by several Native American tribes such as the Algonquian, and the Sioux. The tomahawk quickly became popular with Europeans settlers for its versatility and effectiveness. In the 18th century, the Continental Congress of the United States in a resolution dated July 18, 1775, decreed that militiamen must provide themselves with a sword or Tomahawk in addition to muskets and bayonets.

Though not general issue, the tomahawk was carried into war by soldiers in both WWII and the Korean War. In the mid to late 1960's a Mohawk WWII veteran, Peter Lagana produced and sold battle ready hawks to soldiers fighting in the Vietnam War. Today the tomahawk has experienced a small revival in the military community.

Tomahawks, while still not general issue items, can be found in campaigns in places such as Afghanistan and Iraq.
The versatility of the tomahawk has also begun to be accepted by law enforcement agencies. The tomahawk has made inroads into special operation units as a multipurpose breeching tool. The tomahawk is also the perfect weapon/tool for the outdoorsman in rural or semi-rural areas. The tomahawk does not seem to be

an obvious civilian weapon for urban environments. If you think about it however, it makes for a great home defense weapon and fits nicely in any car.

When you look at the family the hawk comes from we are talking about hatchets, hammers, and small axes, it makes more sense to treat this weapon as what it is rather than pretending it is a stick or a sword.

SINGLE HANDED GRIPS: THE LONG GRIP

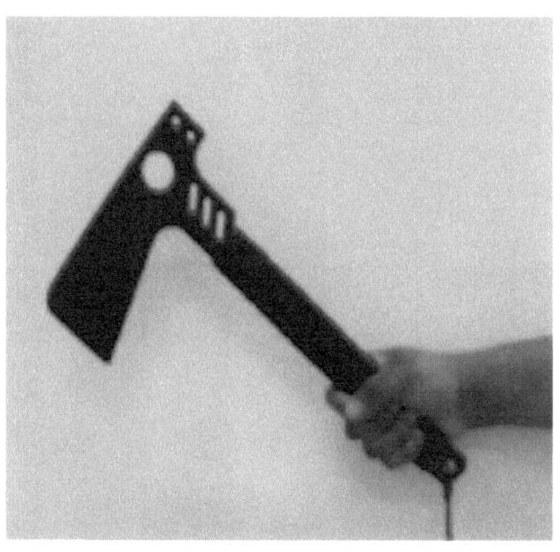

The Forward grip is executed by taking the hawk in the hand in a firm yet relaxed manner. The hand will form a fist around the handle with the thumb resting on the index finger. The edge of the blade should be facing away from the Scout and in alignment with the Scouts middle knuckle line tip up to the sky. Many instructors will advocate a modified version of this grip, often called a saber grip. In the saber grip the Scout's thumb will rest on the spine of the blade. While this gives additional support through strong skeletal alignment, I do not recommend this grip. The reason being that a strong "blade beat", or even inadvertent jamming can easily dislodge the weapon. If this grip is used it should be done so sparingly once the Scout is in the midst of an attack. It should also be noted that the stripping defense methods found in south East Asian martial arts are often less effective against the Heaven grip. The Heaven grip should be used when maximum range is desired as it allows the Scout to more effectively work from the long range.

THE SCOUT STANCE

The scout stance is taken by standing Square with the feet approximately 12 inches apart. The Scout will then take their non-dominant leg and slide it back about 10 inches. The dominant leg will have the foot planted firmly on the ground. The non-dominant leg will be planted on the ball of the foot. The knees should be slightly bent. The hips and shoulders should be in alignment. The torso will be upright, do not crouch. The weapon hand will be held in front of the body at center line. The elbow should be bent with the eye of the hawk facing the opponent. It is crucial when adopting this posture that the Scout keep their entire body behind their extended Hawk. No part of the body should be flush with the Hawk or in front of it. The extended Hawk should be thought of as a shield.

If the enemy wishes to attack any part of the Scout's body they must first contend with the Hawk. Much is made about blading the body for target denial. We feel this is a mistake in blade fighting. One of the key reasons a Scout would blade their body is to establish a structure that is bio-mechanically correct for executing blows and strikes. In weapon fighting the blade does most of the work and we need not adopt a bladed stance in order to deliver effective blows. Also, it is important to note that a bladed body is much easier to flank than a body in the scout stance.

BLOCKING:
The Tomahawk offers great defensive capabilities to the Scout. Because the hawk can be gripped in so many ways and has various striking surfaces, it offers a variety of defensive techniques. Despite the surface used, the Scout will become accustomed to blocking in the four cardinal directions. Those directions are Up, Down, Right, Left.

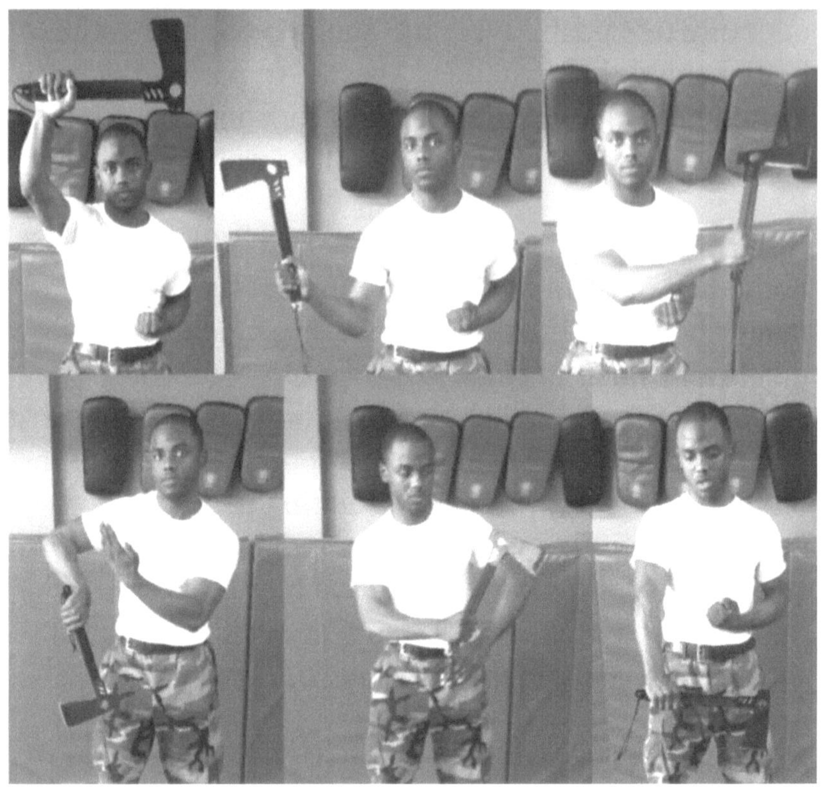

In photos one, two, three and six the Scout will extend their hawk outwards to meet the incoming attack. The Scout will receive the blow on the shaft of their hawk. In photo four and five the Scout will adjust the hawk and cover with the live hand.

OFFENSIVE TECHNIQUES

In this section we will examine the various offensive techniques used in the system. It is important to note that there are several variations of the techniques presented. Only the core techniques will be presented here. The Scout should practice all of these techniques and become proficient and comfortable with their execution.

ONE HANDED CHOP

The one handed chop is executed from the long grip. The chop is a heavy cleaving blow. The chop can be executed with full follow through or by making contact and then rapidly retracting. It must be noted that the chop is just that. A chop. It is not a cut. A "cut" is an awkward and unlikely attack from the long grip.

THE THRUST

To execute the thrust the attack should begin from the chosen guard and extend outwards towards the target for the thrust and then return to the chosen guard with the point of the hawk oriented towards the enemy. A committed thrust should be made with complete follow through, bringing one's mass with them. When making a non-committed thrust the Scout should move their hawk out and back rapidly like a piston.

POMMEL STRIKE

Pommel Strike. The pommel strike is executed by striking with the bottom of the hawk in a hammering motion.

AXING

Axing is a fully committed power cut. The Scout will begin by stepping through with the strong side leg and simultaneously drop the blade from the high position down into their target. As the blade makes contact, the Scout will sink into a deep horse stance allowing their entire body weight to pull through in the attack. At the end of the attack the Scout will allow their attacking forearm to make contact with their thigh. This contact will prevent injury by preventing the Scout from cutting into their leg.

CUTTING PATTERNS

In the art of the blade there is arguably nothing more important than understanding how to effectively move the hawk in slash and thrust action. In our art we use a variety of cutting patterns to teach students the correct lines of attack, fluid motion, and overall comfort in manipulating the blade. The Scout can and should practice all of these angles as outlined. Although originally presented as cutting angels, the arrangement works equally well with thrusting techniques.

1. Vertical upward cut
2. Ascending diagonal cut from left to right
3. Horizontal cut from left to right
4. Descending diagonal cut from left to right
5. Vertical Downward Cut
6. Descending diagonal cut from right to left
7. Horizontal cut from right to left
8. Ascending diagonal cut from right to left

MIND
BODY
SPIRIT

It is important for the warrior scout to recognize that we are more than our bodies and our skills. To be truly balanced one must acknowledge and nurture our minds and spirit also.

The mind can be nourished by reading good books and learning new things everyday. Non-fiction books teach us how to do things. Biographies allow us to learn and be inspired by renowned people everywhere. Even fantasy, fiction and action packed stories teach us things and inspire us on a deeper than surface level. The well-balanced warrior scout should seek to read books or all kinds as well as watch documentaries and videos that inspire and teach.

The spirit is that part of us where the intuition and conscience dwell. It is the part of us that understands deeper things on a level that the body and mind cannot. This part of us is nurtured by reading books like the Bible and other spiritual writings. Be wise what you read in this area. Meditation and prayer are also part of building up our spirits. Listening to our spirit as it warns us by speaking to us about the choices we are about to make before we make them is important. Don't ignore those deep feelings that make you not feel right about a certain person or choice you are about to make.

This section contains things to feed your body, mind and spirit; exercises for the body, stories to inspire the spirit in us, information to feed the mind.

For more books and resources that nurture the body, mind and spirit offered by the authors go to these websites.

TheRavenTribe.com
RavenTactical.com
RavenTalkPodcast.com
MartialBooks.com
WayoftheRaven.net
WalkingSpiritually.com

THE FOUR WARRIORS

The study of Yoga can offer a person many health benefits. Balance, stress relief, limberness and strength among them. From this practice we borrow for our purposes a posture series called "The Four Warriors". The Four Warriors takes the scout through a series of "warrior" postures which offer a simple and brisk routine that can be practices anywhere.

The sequence of postures will help the scout to develop the body in a number of ways. The legs and feet will be put to work, especially the hamstrings and quadriceps. All of the Core muscles will be fully engaged as well. The arms, shoulders and chest will be worked and virtually all stabilizing muscles will come into play throughout the series. Scouts will also work on balance and stability. The body will get a deep stretch and will see improved flexibility of the spine.

The sequence should ideally be done by holding each posture for 4 breaths, with the transitional postures being held for 2 breaths. Scouts should breathe in through their nose slowly for a 4 count, expanding the diaphragm. The breath should be exhaled on a 4 count as well.

WARRIOR ONE

The scout should begin standing with their feet together with hands folded in front. The scout will then execute the first posture. The scout will exhale and step out keeping the feet about 4 ft. apart. The scout will then turn the right foot out at 90 degrees. Next pivot the left foot inwards at a 45-degree angle. Twist your body to left completely Go forward on your left knee making a 90 Degree angle. Extend the other leg completely. Raise both arms up above your head. While looking upward arch your back and stretch. Hold this posture for 5 breathes. The scout will then return to the standing posture and hold it for two breaths.

WARRIOR TWO

The scout will move into the next posture by spreading their legs apart about 4ft. The scout will then turn the right foot out. The other foot will turn inward to make a 45 degree angle. Keep it in the center, facing the front. The scout will then go forward on the right knee making a 90 degree angle. Next turn the neck right and look right. The other leg should extend out while bringing both arms parallel to the floor, stretched wide apart. Hold this posture for 5 breaths. The scout will then return to the standing posture and hold it for two breaths.

WARRIOR THREE

The scout will then return to the standing posture and hold it for two breaths. The scout will move into the next posture by joining their palms and reaching out in front of the body, as they lift the left leg to the rear. Continue to reach the arms forward and the leg to the rear, bringing the body parallel to the ground. Hold this pose for 4 breaths. The scout will then return to the standing posture and hold it for two breaths.

WARRIOR FOUR

The scout will move into the next posture. The scout will stand with their feet three to four feet apart, pointing the left foot forward. The scout will then turn the right foot out. The left hand will slide down to the left. The scout will then reach the right hand upwards towards the sky, arching the back. Hold this pose for 4 breaths.

The scout will then return to the standing posture and hold it for two breaths, finishing the sequence.

FALLING DOWN

By Benjamin Raven Pressley

I stand at the base of towering peaks that stand before me. I look about me as cowering thoughts go through my mind to leave this accursed place and remember it no more.

Yet there is a lion within me that growls and paces about in anger at such thoughts, his hot breath becoming a fire within my bones, and I look to the mountain's height and grit my teeth in holy anger, my gums become white and the taste of blood trickles upon my tongue. As I view the uttermost height lightning strikes and the wind rises to join the thunder in a mocking laughter. Silhouetted by the lightning's strikes I see him, that has hindered my journey, countless times causing me to fall to my undeath just when I reached the heights and would have crossed over this obstacle that dare to hinder my trek of truth. Yet again I reach for its sharpened handholds, I view the craggy heights once more. Once again I see no path before me and determine in my spirit to not look back. “You will not survive the fall this time,” I hear the winds’ raspy voice and I wince as I hear the earth cracking beneath me and I swallow hard as I view the great chasm now opening in the earth beneath me where once I stood. Lightning flashes and its light seems to enhance the chasm’s depths and I know it has opened to receive me should I fall. I hear it cracking once again and flames leap from its depths and the voices of the damned cry their eternal cries of hopelessness. Then I hear his laugh again echoing down the very corridors of my soul. My footing slips as the rock supporting my foot gives away and tumbles down, down, down . . . I cling ever harder to restrain my fall and a cold sweat breaks upon my brow and my heart speeds up and would seemingly leap from my chest. I hide my face against the shear face of the stone that I now cling to as some fearing babe would its mother. I cry a sob forced out by the overcoming prospect of what could have befallen me. The wind blows the tear from my face as I look to the next handhold, my fingertips now white and bleeding, every blood vessel in my hands seem to stand out as if bursting to get out of their prison of flesh. My hands and legs tremble from the strain and I continue to climb …

Then as I look I see my adversary before me and above me, hands on his hips, his blackened robes flapping in the wind, his blackened features as sharpened and craggy as the peaks he defends. He bows slightly to look over the edge and sees me below, within reach if we were standing on the same plane. His mouth salivates in anticipation of striking the final blow. He knows my next step, my next hold I will be within distance for him to kick me into the abyss, to watch me fall as he has before, knowing this time I will not survive the gaping jaws that have opened beneath me. Now within distance I see his cloven hoof lift to kick me below, confident that I shall go down as easily as before and he stomps his hoof down aimed into my face, though weakened from the additional strain of the earths quaking, and the many bouts with fear as I scaled these heights, the lion roars within me, a second wind arises from within and I move my face and move in such a way the evil one loses his balance. I secure myself quickly, as I move from his hoove's path and reach, with a strength that proceeds from within not totally my own. The black hearted one falls as if tossed by some supernatural arm and struggles uselessly beating at the air, with his arms and legs as if to reach for the salvation that is not there. His screams are piercing and full of the ultimate terror of his sure and ever confirmation of his fears.

I cling with one hand to my last hold, my footing holding on by I know not what and well springs of relief and almost unbelieving joy surge up within as I view the last of his descent and for only a brief moment view the flame leaping higher as if receiving a new and volatile fuel, then the earth closes its mouth and the air seems ever cooler than before. I stand and stare for only a brief second and hardly swallow, when

I turn, startled by another presence, at first not knowing what to expect. A hand reaches for me, ivory and polished, somehow, though not knowing him, I trust this one and I extend forth my hand, our fingertips touch only briefly, yet in this short moment I feel warmth spreading through my body and every muscle, nerve, and fiber of my being seems to relax. Then I feel his strong grip upon my hand as I am lifted the final leg of the journey. I behold him and cannot take my eyes from his face. I am utterly undone, and every emotion I have ever felt swells up from within me and I am drawn to him like a little child, I fall upon his breast, he embraces me, and then I feel complete, more complete than I ever thought possible to be, I cry, a cry of relief, as all that is unlike him flows from my eyes, clean at last as I hear him say with words that express the deepest love, a deeper love I have never heard expressed as he says to me, "Well done." and hear his tears of joy as he says once again, " Well done."

Want to read more stories like these? Check out Raven's book
THE TRAVELER'S JOURNAL

WARRIOR WORDS

WORDS TO LIVE BY

This section contains some of our favorite inspiring quotes. The mind is so important to keep right in every situation. Body follows mind. Meditating on wise and inspiring quotes can help you accomplish that.

"Time is asymmetrical. We can know about the past, but cannot change it. We can influence the future, but cannot know it. We are all locked together in the split, split-second that is the present. The literal time machine of our dreams still waits for its own invention."—Steven M. Watts

"There are always the quiet revolutionaries who give thanks for grace in the unexpected. There are always the real revolutionaries who know this overthrows all the pressing dark. There are, even now, the revolutionaries who know what they were saved for. They choose to give glory with the breaths given. They choose to be married to amazement because only amazing grace divorces souls from the dark." —Ann Voskamp

"Life offers us the opportunity to become a "Spiritual Warrior." A Warrior is one who bravely goes into those dark areas within themselves. It takes great courage, stamina, and endurance to become a "Spiritual Warrior." The path is narrow, the terrain rough and rocky. You will walk alone: through the dark caves, up steep climbs, and through the dense thick forest. You will meet your dark side. The faces of fear, deceit, and sadness all await your arrival. No one can take this journey but you. There comes a time in each of our lives, when we are given the choice to follow this path. Should we decide to embark on this journey we can never turn back?.... Our lives are changed forever on this journey. There are many different places we can choose to slip into and hide. But the path goes on. The "Spiritual Warrior" stays the course, wounded at times, exhausted, and out of energy. Many times, the Warrior will struggle back to his feet to take only a few steps before falling again. Rested, he forges on, continuing the treacherous path...One day... the battle, loneliness, and desperate fights are over..The warrior has fought the courageous fight. New energy now fills the Warrior....A new path is now laid before him....A gentler path filled with the inner-knowing of one who has personal empowerment. With their personal battle won, they are filled with joy....A new awareness that they are one with the Spirit, as they go forth to show others the way.....They are not permitted to walk the path for others....They can only love, guide, and be a living example of the truth of their being...."

-Ana Marie

"When the power of love overcomes the love of power the world will know peace."
-Jimi Hendrix

"Freedom lies in being bold."
— Robert Frost

"Whatever you do, you need courage. Whatever course you decide upon, there is always someone to tell you that you are wrong. There are always difficulties arising that tempt you to believe your critics are right. To map out a course of action and follow it to an end requires some of the same courage that a soldier needs. Peace has its victories, but it takes brave men and women to win them."
— Ralph Waldo Emerson

"Do every single thing you can to protect yourself, your family, and your country."
-William Goldberg

"Courage is grace under pressure."
— Ernest Hemingway

"Life is mostly froth and bubble,
Two things stand like stone.
Kindness in another's trouble,
Courage in your own."
— Adam Lindsay Gordon

"Have courage for the great sorrows of life and patience for the small ones; and when you have laboriously accomplished your daily task, go to sleep in peace. God is awake."
— Victor Hugo

"Believe you can and you're halfway there."
— Theodore Roosevelt
There is no substitution for experience.
- Robert James Marella

"A man with outward courage dares to die; a man with inner courage dares to live."
— Lao Tzu

"Courage. Kindness. Friendship. Character. These are the qualities that define us as human beings, and propel us, on occasion, to greatness."
— R.J. Palacio

"Keep in mind that many people have died for their beliefs; it's actually quite common. The real courage is in living and suffering for what you believe."
— Christopher Paolini

"Sometimes it's what you don't do that makes you who you are."
-Phillip Brooks

"If what that man did in his life, makes the blood pulse through the body of others, and makes them believe deeper in something larger than life, then his essence, his spirit, will be immortalized by the storytellers, by the loyalty, by the memory, of those who honor him and make whatever the man did live forever." --James Helwig

"Without fear there cannot be courage."
— Christopher Paolini

"So comes snow after fire, and even dragons have their endings."
— J.R.R. Tolkien, The Hobbit

"Life is made of so many moments that mean nothing. Then one day, a single moment comes along to define every second that comes after. Such moments are tests of courage, of strength."
— Sabaa Tahir

"Man cannot discover new oceans unless he has the courage to lose sight of the shore."
— André Gide

"You can build walls all the way to the sky and I will find a way to fly above them. You can try to pin me down with a hundred thousand arms, but I will find a way to resist. And there are many of us out there, more than you think. People who refuse to stop believing. People who refuse to come to earth. People who love in a world without walls, people who love into hate, into refusal, against hope, and without fear."— Lauren Oliver

"Courage is not simply one of the virtues but the form of every virtue at the testing point, which means at the point of highest reality. "
— C.S. Lewis

"One hard day of work proves you have heart. But day after day is what proves you have maturity and commitment."
-Dwayne Johnson

"Knowledge speaks, but wisdom listens."
-Jimi Hendrix

"Whether we are driven toward the stronghold of God because of problems or passion, there is a holy place where the divine presence becomes our shelter."
-The Shelter of the Most High By Francis Frangipane

"Zeal unaccompanied by wisdom eventually becomes its own god. It compels us toward expectations that are unrealistic."
-The Shelter of the Most High By Francis Frangipane

"People are the story they tell themselves."
-Joseph Falkinburg

"Real compassion is not a kind of luxurious pity where you look down on others from a distance and give them a little gift to make them temporarily feel better. It is a complete and intense involvement, like being cast into the middle of a blazing fire."
-Karmapa

"We can see that we ourselves are actually a part of others; and we can see that others are also a part of us."--Karmapa

"We don't know who we are until we are connected to someone else"
-Tara Teller

"Every act of conscious learning requires the willingness to suffer an injury to one's self-esteem. That is why young children, before they are aware of their own self-importance, learn so easily."
-Thomas Szasz

"Being bitter and dwelling on past hurt only gives it power over us and does not change the past. It only takes away our energy that we could be using to sustain a better future."—Benjamin Raven Pressley

ABOUT THE AUTHORS

FERNAN VARGAS

Mr. Vargas is a lifelong martial artist who currently holds a Menkyo Kaiden in Bushi Satori Ryu as well as black belts and instructor rankings in Kuntao, Silat, Kuntaw, Jujutsu and Hapkido. As a certified Law Enforcement Defensive Tactics Instructor, Mr. Vargas has taught defensive tactics to law enforcement Scouts at the local, state, and federal level, as well as security Scouts, military personnel and private citizens from around the United States and foreign nations such as Canada, Italy, and Spain. Mr. Vargas has developed programs which have been approved by the Police training and Standards Board of several states, and adopted by agencies such as the Pentagon Force protection Agency. Additionally, organizations such as the Fraternal Order of Law Enforcement and the International Academy of Executive Protection Agents have given formal endorsements of the programs developed by Mr. Vargas. Mr. Vargas has been an instructor at the prestigious International Law Enforcement Educators & Trainers Association International Conference (ILEETA).

Fernan Vargas is a current Safety Patrol Leader and Trainer for the Chicago Chapter of the Guardian Angels Safety Patrol. He is the only American to be granted the title of Soma de Cutel by Grand Master Gilberto Pauciullo and the Instituto per le Tradisioni Marziali Italiane. Mr. Vargas has also been awarded the honorific title of Master Knife Instructor by his Sifu David Siewert. and the designation of Mater At Arms by Ernest Emerson and the Order of the Black Shamrock.

Mr. Vargas was named Trainer of the Year 2011 by the Alliance of Guardian Angels and has been inducted in several halls of fame for his instruction of Defensive Tactics and Combatives. Mr. Vargas has been inducted into several Martial Arts Halls of Fame and has been awarded the Presidential Service Award and the Shinja Buke Ryu Humanitarian Award for service to the community.

To contact Vargas and view his books and other resources available be sure and visit his websites at:

www.TheRavenTribe.com

www.RavenTactical.com

www.RavenTalkPodcast.com

www.MartialBooks.com

BENJAMIN 'RAVEN' PRESSLEY

Benjamin 'RAVEN' Pressley practices and teaches the skills of the past; primitive, survival and wilderness living skills practiced for generations by Native Americans and aboriginal peoples all over the world.

Raven teaches all ages. He is well known from the organization he and a friend founded, called *TRIBE.* *TRIBE* was a great success. *TRIBE* was a successful network, school and a resource that brought together people practicing primitive skills all over the U.S., with membership in Guam, Canada, Spain, Mexico, England and New Guinea. Raven continues to teach at schools, colleges, civic organizations, *Scouts, Y-Indian Guides, Royal Rangers, YMCA*, museums and historical sites. He has written and self published many books on various primitive, survival and wilderness living skills. He is also a writer for magazines, such as: *Backwoodsman, Wilderness Way* and *American Survival Guide*. Benjamin has been a Staff Editor for *Backwoodsman* magazine and the Southeastern U.S. Field Editor for *Wilderness Way* magazine. He has played in instructional video curriculum and educational television movies depicting life in our country between 1750-1790.

Raven also has experience in several styles of martial arts though he holds no black belt rank in any of the arts. He is a warrior that follows the path influenced by his martial arts training and disciplines learned therein.

Raven is also a spiritual guide and philosopher. His spiritual beliefs are very balanced for all and draws upon his Cherokee heritage and the teachings of Jesus Christ. Raven believes there is a balance to be struck between our mental, physical, social and spiritual selves. Raven believes all people regardless of gender, race, etc. should be treated equally and taught to reach their full potential.

To contact Raven and view his books and other resources available be sure and visit his websites at:

For Survival Skills: WayoftheRaven.net

For Spiritual Guidance: WalkingSpiritually.com

OTHER WORKS BY BENJAMIN RAVEN PRESSLEY

Available at
WayoftheRaven.net and
WalkingSpiritually.com

◇ **Can You Survive?** --- A complete guide to wilderness survival skills

◇ **RAVENQUEST**---Raven's 7 volume fantasy fiction series

◇ **The Traveler's Journal**---A collection of inspiring original short stories and poems.

◇ **True Spirituality**---A non-religious look at what true spirituality is and is not.

◇**Touching God**---Understanding what being in a relationship with God is all about. Prayer, intercession and meditation.

◇ **Are We Making This Too Hard?** ---A series of studies based on the Holy Bible.

◇ **Things I Wish Someone Had Told Me When I Became A Christian**---An objective non-religious look into what the Bible actually says about following the teachings of Jesus Christ.

◇ **Also** many other titles available on Kindle

OTHER WORKS BY FERNAN VARGAS

Available at
RavenTactical.com

- Way of the Raven Blade Combatives Vol. 1-8
- Way of the Raven Tomahawk Combatives Vol. 1-2
- Way of the Raven Telescopic Baton Vol. 1-2
- Cuchillo Corvo: Combat Knife of Chile
- Knuckle Duster: A Guide to Brass Knuckles
- Surviving the Active Killer
- The Great American War Club
- Native American Blade Combatives
- Things You Should know In Case I am Not Here to Tell You
- Little Dragon Dojo: Martial Arts for Kids
- Self Defense 101
- Fire Arm Defense and Retention Tactics
- The Knife Fighting of Cold Steel
- USMC Knife-Counter Knife Combatives
- It's Not A lot, It's Silat
- Rikugun Ninjutsu: Shinobi Iri and Inton Jutsu

www.ingramcontent.com/pod-product-compliance
Ingram Content Group UK Ltd.
Pitfield, Milton Keynes, MK11 3LW, UK
UKHW041938190726
13854UKWH00004B/1653